The Actor's *Other* Career Book

Using Your Chops

to Survive and Thrive

Lisa Mulcahy

**ALLWORTH
PRESS**
NEW YORK

for my father,
William Mulcahy

© 2006 Lisa Mulcahy

09 08 07 06 05   5 4 3 2 1

Published by Allworth Press
An imprint of Allworth Communications, Inc.
10 East 23rd Street, New York, NY 10010

Cover design by Derek Bacchus
Interior design by Joan O'Connor
Page composition/typography by Integra Software Services, Pvt. Ltd., Pondicherry, India
Cover photo: *www.paulgodwin.com*

ISBN: 1-58115-453-4

Library of Congress Cataloging-in-Publication Data

Mulcahy, Lisa.
   The actor's other career book: using your chops to survive & thrive/Lisa Mulcahy.
       p.   cm.
   Includes bibliographical references and index.
   ISBN 1-58115-453-4 (pbk.)
   1. Acting—Vocational guidance.   2. Career changes.   I. Title.

   PN2055.M85 2006
   792.02'8023—dc22

                                                            2006016400

Printed in the United States of America

acknowledgements

acknowledgements

I enthusiastically thank and praise the following fine folks for the invaluable help they provided during the evolution of this book:

As ever, I express my utmost admiration and appreciation to Tad Crawford and Nicole Potter-Talling at Allworth Press, for their incredible support, infallible guidance, and wonderful trust. I salute Michael Madole for the great work he does on all of my books, and give special thanks for his special contributions on this project. I give my great appreciation to Jessica Rozler, for her always-terrific expertise. I also pay my respects to the entire Allworth staff, whose professionalism is simply peerless.

To the superb artists/professionals interviewed in this book who so generously allowed me into their work lives, I'm profoundly grateful. Your insight, candor, amazing emotional intelligence, and generosity are invaluable gifts to readers everywhere. All my best to Buzz Alexander, Sherri Allen, Bob Alter, Cooper Bates, Bob Bergen, Nicole Bigham, Brian Carpenter, Sean Cercone, Gil Christner, David Christopher, Megan Cole, Randy Farias, Amy Dolan Fletcher, Leanna Foglia, Laura Giannelli, Daena Giardella, Constantine Gregory, Patrick Grimes, Ayo Haynes, Lora Heller, Annie Hughes, Ellen Kaplan, Sheila Kelley, Douglas Kondziolka, Kenny Kramer, Shannon Kringen, Lara Kulpa, Brian Keith Lewis, Rita Litton, Amanda Malby, Carol Mannes, Michael McGarty, The Naked Cowboy, Steve Nevil, James O'Regan, Darryl Palmer, Gail Parker, Deb Pickman, Jill Perry, Dennis Rees, Victor Rivers, Paul Salos, Sebastian Saraceno, David Shookhoff, Jim Sterling, Tammy Tanner, Samantha von Sperling, Elaina Vrattos, JT Wagner, Debbie Williams, Kelly Wohlford, and Craig Wroe.

For their kind assistance in helping me arrange and facilitate interviews, and supplying me with great supplementary information, many thanks go to Melissa Garland, Jennifer from The Naked Cowboy.com, Daphne Ortiz at Much & House Public Relations, Bryanne Jones of Compassion and Choices, Jane Salos, Bill Ware of the William Ware Agency, and the Turtle Lane Playhouse.

I would like to thank Tim Harley and Arlene Palmer for their terrific contributions.

I would also like to express my appreciation to Tom Dangilli.

To Kathy Schrier and Patch Schwadron of the Actors' Work Program, you are the "guardian angels" of this project. I'm so grateful for the time and energy you gave me, the amazing good wishes and wonderful observations you've provided, the fabulous folks you've introduced me to, and most of all, the vital work you do every day on behalf of your clients.

I owe a huge debt to two of the theater's late, great artists, Bob Fosse and Michael Bennett, for their respective influences on this project. I was fortunate to watch documentary footage of both masters working with actors during the formative stages of the film *All That Jazz* (Fosse) and the play *A Chorus Line* (Bennett). The respect they showed for their actors' histories and input was a great inspiration to me indeed.

For outstanding technical know-how, I would like to thank Geoff Grammel and Johanne Cimon of The Most Office in Fitchburg, Massachusetts, whose skills are truly tremendous.

To the Brandeis University theater community, you provided both the spark and the foundation. A very special thanks as always to Ted Kazanoff and to Edward Albee for teaching me the true essentials of theater.

All my gratitude to the wonderful theater pros I've worked with on the New York City scene. To my posse of friends, I love your loyalty.

To my lovely family, the extended Mulcahy and Kelly clans, you are simply the greatest!

I would like to give a very special thank you to my gorgeous and brilliant cousins Lori Card, Tina Cooley, and Shannon Flematti for the awesome New York City inspiration they provided for this book!

Most of all, I thank my beautiful mom Joan Mulcahy, and send her all the love in the world.

—LISA MULCAHY

contents

contents

introduction
the successful actor's mindset

What's the one thing that every living, breathing actor everywhere wants more than anything? It's work, plain and simple. If the ink on your diploma's still wet, you're racking your brain and pounding the pavement, hunting down that first gig. Even If you're the current toast of Broadway, you're no doubt thinking, "What am I gonna do next?" Which is only natural. Making a consistent living at the craft of acting is extremely tough to do, no matter who you are.

The reality is, traditional performance work is a scarce commodity, and always will be. An actor seeking work in any major city, be it in stage, film, or TV, is bound to be discouraged by the huge number of competitors they face per potential job. Complicating matters further, if you don't live in New York or Los Angeles, you're pretty much invisible as far as most high-caliber casting agents are concerned—plus, in terms of parts, the pickins' are probably mighty slim wherever you do happen to live. Then there's the money angle. Unless your name is Jim Carrey or Cameron Diaz, you're not raking in the big bucks—even if you are a regularly working actor, a good deal of your earnings probably goes toward paying your union insurance, and you no doubt live on a very tight budget.

And don't forget the happiness factor. If you do get lucky and get a role, is it really satisfying your artistic impulse? Playing a talking carrot in a frozen veggie commercial probably isn't making that happen. Are you doing anything to make the world a better place? Many actors really feel a calling toward social contribution, but can't really figure out how to achieve it through work as an extra in *Dude, Where's My Car?*

So you really have two choices, it would seem. Your first option: continue to suffer nobly, hoping that one day, lightning will strike and you'll finally catch that big break—not very proactive OR practical. So let's talk about your second option: expand your mind! Great permanent or temporary jobs for actors exist all around you. You can apply for them, network toward them, or create them on your own—you've got the power to shape your career, and improve your quality of life, right this very second.

Where is the work plentiful? In corporate America. In education. In social outreach. At tourist attractions, in the living history field, in physical fitness, in media, and more. Consistently employed actors who take control of their professional circumstances make it their business to think outside of the box, figure out how the skills they've developed as performers can be translated to diverse fields, and go for a better life.

Uh, oh—sounds like I'm talking about a career change. I am, and I'm not. It's VERY freaky for most actors to contemplate other work because acting is so entwined with their self-esteem, and probably has been since they could talk. Here's a major truth, though—most actors who do other work, whether it's a solid sideline occupation or any entirely fresh job apart from conventional acting, continue to call themselves actors. Many continue to act. You'll meet over fifty performers who've successfully sought other work in this book alone, and EVERY SINGLE ONE OF THEM STILL CONSIDERS HIM OR HERSELF A FULL-FLEDGED ACTOR.

This fact is an extremely crucial point; in fact, it's the most important thing I learned in researching and writing this book. Working in another field only widens your scope and experience as a person, and that makes you a better actor, whether you perform again tomorrow or twenty years from now.

So how do these successful actors get the steady work, good money, and sense of personal pride and accomplishment that YOU are longing for? There are a variety of traits I've noted that actors pursuing satisfying work have in common. Let's go through them one by one.

THEY SEEK SUPPORT

The Actors' Work Program (AWP) is a highly lauded resource that many actors in this book tell me truly changed their lives. AWP is part of the Actors' Fund of America, and its purpose is to provide comprehensive counseling, training, tuition assistance, and job search and placement support. Over 9,000 entertainment industry pros have used the program over the past decade, and gotten fantastic results.

Kathy Schrier, AWP's managing director, is an extremely supportive, informed, and experienced professional. Let's get her take on how she applies her skills to AWP, how her own accomplished background informs her work today, and the realities of career change.

Kathy Schrier: "My academic background is in labor relations; I spent most of my career in the labor movement, in the field of labor education, working education, adult education, in doing two things. One was as a direct trainer of union members. Through all that, I ran an employment and training program for the municipal workers in New York City, and at the time, it was the largest union-based training program in the United States. The bulk of the work was developing programs to help the membership in terms of career development and upgrading.

"My passion and love has always been theater and the arts. I spent a lot of time even in the academic world learning about labor relations and the performing arts. I'd always wanted to work for the arts; my first job was with American Ballet Theatre.

"When the Actors' Work Program started in 1986, it was not part of the Actors' Fund of America, it started as a committee of Actors Equity. Around 1990 or so, the person who ran the program contacted me, because of my work at the union, for help and guidance. I got onto the advisory board; AWP was by this time an independent program. The program merged with the Actors' Fund in 1997; I left my old job in 1998, did some consulting, and my first job was needs assessment for AWP. I was offered a year appointment, and have been here ever since.

"Our mission is not about transition. Most people in the entertainment industry need to find a parallel second career that complements what they do in the entertainment industry. What we're really about is helping people find balance between their entertainment industry career, no matter how they define that, and their parallel secondary career.

"There is no other group of workers in this country that has the type of work that we do in the entertainment industry. The closest is construction, where people go from job to job, but those jobs tend to be longer in length, and at least in this point in history, there seems to be a lot of work. Even in times of high employment, and we are at a time of extremely high employment in the entertainment industry, there are still many, many, especially actors, who are not working. So what we're about is working with individuals to figure out what other work they can do that is meaningful, that gets the endorphins going, just like being on a stage and in front of a camera.

"The support and the networking (at AWP) are on many, many levels. In [our] orientation, everyone will say the same thing: I'm tired of cater-waiting, I'm tired of going on the road. We sometimes hear from people we've always thought of as successful. They'll say something like 'I've been doing this Broadway musical for the past ten years and I can't stand it anymore.' Or 'I've worked a lot of Off-Broadway contracts, and it doesn't pay the rent.' And those people who have not had what we normally think of as commercial success really start to wonder 'Ohh, what is this business about?' So what happens in that initial orientation usually is that everyone begins to get a sense of community and validation, not only from us, but from their peers, a sense that what I'm going through is not that different than what everybody else is going through.

"The reality of work is what you can do for the employer, not what the employer can do for you. When [actors new to the program] look at work, they look at solely whether it is going to complement or fit in to my ability to go to auditions, which they absolutely must do. But that's not how you get a job. You get a job by not only selling yourself, but really realizing that there's a fit. It's OK to be desperate, but it's not OK to take any job.

"I think the most important message is to let [actors] know that this is healthy and OK if you're beginning to think about other [work]."

Patricia "Patch" Schwadron, AWP's career counseling supervisor, grew up in the theater herself, as her mother was assistant to Adrian Hall at Trinity Rep. A classical dancer who had to stop performing for health reasons, Schwadron has a background in journalism and public relations. She took a job with Susan W. Miller MA, a career counselor in LA, and found herself fascinated by person-to-person counseling. She got her degree in educational career counseling, and worked in career counseling at St. John's University before coming to AWP. Schwadron's past achievements make her perfectly suited to help her clients develop their full potential; this is how she does it.

Patch Schwadron: "First, there's the self-assessment piece: what are my skills? What has been my experience? What are my values? Where do my interests lie? What do I care about? Then, how do I take that assessment process and move forward with it?

"Each person is at a different stage of development, a different stage of life, with different needs. For a small portion of the people who come here, transitioning solidly 100 percent to a new career is their agenda, and we're certainly here to support someone who is interested in and ready to do that. We're really all about making whatever work you do consistent with who you are. That's the nature of our respect for the artist; we understand that what is to be a self-interested artist in this country is to say, 'My work is who I am.' We also feel that everybody in the United States of America should be saying 'My work reflects who I am,' but we have this population, which starts out by saying that. If you start out at the age of two or four or ten by saying, 'I must express myself or I'll die,' to recognize that you need to CHANGE how you do that is very loaded. It's a very emotional, scary process to say, 'I have to change who I am and what I do, and I risk losing who I really feel I am at the core.' There's a tremendous amount of holding of that that goes on here. We have seventeen to thirty new members every Monday; after orientation, people say, 'Thank God, there's a place that understands what I'm feeling!'

"There's an enormous skill set that people develop by being actors and in the theater business that transfers to a wide range of other occupational settings. I get people on Monday who say to me, 'All I do is act.' And I say to them, 'You have 75 to 80 percent of the skill sets that are needed in the world of work. Now, we need to help you figure out where you want to go with that wonderful tool kit you've got, and how do you adapt and enhance what you've already developed in order to be effective and creative and engaged in something that's going to take better care of you.'

"What changes do you feel you have to make in order to be resilient and be creative? How do you define that? What the organization does is create programs that support people who are ready to take one step or another. We talk about readiness here a lot. Readiness is a big piece. I've been here six years now, and have clients I've known for six years, who were clients of the AWP prior to my [arrival]. We've been able to really see longitudinally what it takes for people to change. It takes time. There's no magic. They come in and say, 'Give me a job and fix my life,' and we say, 'No. You need to do some work, you need to do some thinking, you need to do some self-exploration, and do it in small steps.' This is experiential learning. The endorphin goal sometimes doesn't come for a while. There's a career theorist in San Francisco who talks about work like falling in love. He'll say, 'Did you marry the first person you fell in love with?' They'll say, 'Thank God, no.' 'Did it feel the same the second time you fell in love?' 'No.' You're not going to have that same experience of, this is it, this is who I am, I identify, I bond with it, like teenage romantic love. As an adult, your choices are more complex, there are pluses and minuses, there's a resistance to change that's completely normal. We're really here to say to people, 'Hang in there, let's keep looking at it. How did that feel? What worked, what didn't work. This is a process, this takes time, and we're here to support you through that time.'

"We're so high energy. We're so excited as an organization about helping people. It's like, we have the key!"

Smart actors use such an excellent resource to help identify their strengths and help them go far indeed.

THEY GET REAL

Successful, gainfully employed actors don't have pie-in-the-sky ideas about their true value. The mega-achievers in this book rarely care about being famous (although several of them ARE famous) with the notable exception of The Naked Cowboy (see chapter 13)—who very shrewdly works on his fame as a way to build his brand and message. They care about enjoying the work they do, day by day, minute by minute, and how they can use that work to help themselves and other people.

THEY ENJOY THE THRILL OF THE HUNT

The actors who truly do well for themselves career-wise become very skilled at research. They also don't put all their eggs in one basket, pursuing a variety of potential jobs before choosing one specifically. When it comes to negotiation, too, they're not shy about asking for—and getting—the exact terms they want.

THEY HAVE A LIGHTBULB MOMENT

This could be a huge, sudden revelation that their life has got to change for the better. Could be a feeling of discontent that creeps in over time, then totally overwhelms them. Actors who make constructive shifts see a financial crisis, a lost job, or a life tragedy as a positive in the long run, in that it's the one incident they can point to that made them get their acts together.

THEY DON'T HAVE UNREALISTIC EXPECTATIONS

Rome wasn't built in a day, and your career won't be, either. Winners understand that they must lay the bricks under a new profession, in order to have a firm and lasting foundation to their lives. Many of the actors in this book have worked years to achieve their successes, and they're OK with that fact of life.

THEY DIG DIALOGUE

Actors who have found true harmony in their work have paid lots of attention to those who've gone before them in a field, and generally have asked those folks lots of savvy questions. They also want to share the hard-earned information they've gathered on the way up with those looking to make a career change as they did. The actors you're about to meet are living proof of this—they're here to help you!

So why not make their effort truly count? A great way to get the most out of the profiles, experience, and advice you're about to absorb is to make this book an interactive experience. Grab a pen and pad if you want, and let's do some brainstorming.

Write down your answers to the following questions first.

1. What would I like to change about my current work situation as an actor?
2. What scares me the most about making a career change?
3. What excites me most about making a career change?
4. What traits do I bring to the table that will make it easy to secure new, better work?
5. What hobbies or interests could I possibly turn into a career?
6. How important is making a lot of money to me, really?

7. What's my ideal annual income that I feel I could realistically achieve with new work?
8. Am I really a people person deep down?
9. Do I actually prefer working on my own?
10. Do I honestly have the discipline to be a freelancer, or am I better off working for a specific company?
11. Am I satisfied that I am making a social difference in the world?
12. If not, how might I go about making a social difference with new work?
13. How much time and energy am I truly willing to put into a job search right now?
14. Am I a good multitasker?
15. Could I see myself pursuing a number of diverse jobs or career goals at the same time?
16. Am I a practical person, or is my head too much in the clouds?
17. How much positive reinforcement from others do I really need in order to be happy?
18. What are three jobs I could see myself being content doing?
19. Do I need additional education or training for those positions?
20. How much more time am I willing to stick out my current unhappy situation?

Obviously, you might want to take a bit of time to consider these queries, as they're pretty in-depth. Or you may be so fired up to wipe the slate clean in your life that you'll start scribbling responses right away. The point is, start thinking. The answers are already inside you—it's just a matter of getting real with yourself, and getting them out on the table.

When you're reading this book, I'd love it if you felt the urge to note the specific bits of advice actors give that you really respond to, or write down why you might be interested in a particular career outlined in the book, or jot down why you liked a particular actor so very much. Doing this will help you further identify your own goals, tastes, and qualities that you might share with someone you admire. It's all about being as self-aware as possible. Once you truly know yourself, your potential is limitless, your energy is endless, and your faith in the future is unshakable.

Let the actors you're about to meet inspire and move you—then get to work on your own success story.

one
living history

A good actor needs to maintain a healthy respect for the past in order to interpret a character well. Think about it: you're often called upon to research a long-ago decade in time in order to authentically convey you're living in it onstage. Or you customarily create a back story history for your character, to help you access his/her emotional make-up. It all boils down to curiosity: the best actors have loads of it, and learning about unfamiliar people, places, and periods is a great way to keep your senses sharp.

It's no surprise, then, that actors pursuing another career are often drawn to jobs that allow them to indulge their need to know. Work having to do with historic times is very plentiful for those with a creative background, and I'm not just talking about playing a Pilgrim during that weeklong walking tour of Plymouth Rock. The talented individuals I spotlight in this chapter have found their professional passions through a deep fascination with days gone by—maybe you can, too.

THE TIME TRAVELER

It's 1891, and Patrick Grimes has dressed in his finest Victorian suit this morning. He strides through the historic mansion he calls home, pausing to appreciate the seaside view before greeting his fellow aristocrats at 9:30 AM. Then he and his fancy friends—plus their servants, of course—begin to graciously welcome hundreds of visitors to his abode, showing off its breathtaking architecture, impressing the throngs with its gorgeous furnishings, and charming them with local gossip.

After a full day of entertaining, by 5:00 PM, Grimes changes clothes and morphs straight into the Roaring Twenties. Tonight, he's hosting a swanky soiree for another 140 guests, including F. Scott and Zelda Fitzgerald and Cole Porter.

By eleven PM? Grimes has fast-forwarded to the twenty-first century, and is spending some quality time watching Jon Stewart on *The Daily Show*.

Is Grimes reliving an episode of the old TV series *Quantum Leap*? No—it's all part of a day's work for him at Astors' Beechwood Mansion in Newport, Rhode Island. This meticulously maintained living history museum employs the services of talented thespians who, in character as Victorians, give tours and interact face-to-face with visitors. Popular special events held at the mansion include a recreated party with the passengers of the Titanic, a thrilling, chilling murder mystery, or a rollicking night in a speakeasy.

Grimes started at Beechwood in 1996 as a performer. How did it all happen? "I went to the University of Northern Colorado and got a degree in acting," he explains. "From there, I started my own comedy improv group, Some Crazy Garbage, with some friends—that name comes from a They Might Be Giants song, by the way. We were doing OK, and we had aspirations to start our own film company, and we talked about where we were going to move to do that. The decision was made that we should all pack up and move from Colorado to Oregon—that Portland was the place to start a film company, for some reason.

"Really, what we liked about the area was that Portland had lots of little independent theaters, and these had the ability to show digital movies. So we could produce short movies on our computers, and then we'd have the ability to actually show them on a screen. That all got delayed when one friend from our group, Dylan Paschke, got a job at the Beechwood Mansion. They were looking for men, and Dylan said, 'I know a few more guys who would be great at this.' So Beechwood gave me a call. I was given two weeks to get my act together and move to Rhode Island. I didn't have to audition, because they had a guy lined up who backed out, so they were stuck, and went pretty much on Dylan's recommendation."

Upon his arrival in Newport, Grimes was thrown into the fire—or "Victorian Boot Camp," as it's fondly referred to by mansion staffers. "We went through two weeks of really intense training," he remembers. "It's tons of history, which you've got to then digest and personalize, so you can relate it as present-day fact, and how it affects your particular person, whether you're a real-life character from the 1890s, or a servant character, who is pretty much created entirely by the actor. It was a very different experience, insofar as you're right there—there's no fourth wall. It's totally interactive—you're pressin' palms, you're learnin' names, and you're completely immersed as this character, trying to bring everyone who's shown up to where you are.

"My first character was John G. Sebastian IV, who died on the Titanic. That particular year, they decided to do two characters for everyone—we all had an aristocrat character and a servant character. It made things easier for everyone, because you got to go from lighting $100 bills to get your cigars going to polishing someone's shoes. You couldn't get too big for your britches!"

Grimes says he continues to research his roles quite intensely. "This work requires constant maintenance. Every actor gets a great big binder, which is filled with the biographical information about his real-life character, and also a ton of US and world history. Current events of the time period you're portraying are broken down by month. Everyone is encouraged to brush up, because you're doing so much—you're performing in the house five days a week, which means you could be seeing in the neighborhood of 5,000 people per week. To keep yourself from going crazy, you need to keep everything fresh. We also further storylines for people by publishing our own edition of the *Town Topics*, which was a gossip rag of the time. In that we publish articles from the original *Town Topics*, plus articles that pertain from the *New York Times*, the *New York Post*, the *Newport News*—things pulled from archives that keep everyone abreast of things that happened. The Astor Place disaster building collapse, for example—you can talk about something like that, asking, 'Do you know if any bodies have been pulled from the rubble?' to anyone you meet on the tour."

Grimes loves the instant gratification his job provides. "This can be so much more satisfying than a regular acting job. You're right there with people, interacting with them, and when you get a great group that's interested in playing along, you learn their names, they learn your name, it's great to know they left having a great time," he enthuses. "Then other times, you get the school groups filled with disaffected teens, which can be completely exhausting and frustrating. But that's dealing with teenagers, and what can you do? We were all miserable little turds at one point in our lives."

Grimes doubles as production manager at the mansion, so he is responsible for large amounts of scheduling and logistics, in addition to his tour duties. "I run morning call, where we all meet to discuss whether any big groups are coming in, whether we're closing early because there's a big event in the evening," he reports. "We talk about reservations and where we stand for big events. We get warmed up, and decide what order we are in for the day—everyone knows what particular section they're in, but they don't know the order they're running in, so if there's two or three people working a particular house section, sometimes they have to play rock, paper, scissors. This is a huge portion of what we do here at Beechwood!

"Then we do everything to make sure the previous evening's event didn't leave empty cocktail glasses or smashed strawberries under the furniture. Then we open up, and every half hour, a new group will spend between forty-five minutes and an hour being shown around the house. It changes when we go to our Christmas tour schedule, when we only do three to four tours a day—they're an hour long."

Grimes's hours and workload varies. "If I don't have an event in the evening, I'm here from 9:00 AM to about 5:30 PM. In the summer, I can be here from 9:00 AM to 10:00 PM. This takes the ability to compartmentalize. If you had a really crappy tour day, you can't let that affect you, because you have a murder mystery or a speakeasy in the evening.

"As far as actual performance time during the day, they split up the house, so you either do the first floor or the second floor. On the first floor, you're with a group for about twenty, twenty-five minutes, and you're only doing that once an hour. You have thirty minutes down between each. It creates a lot of unique opportunities; you get really good at croquet. I have that game DOWN!"

The pace is generally pretty hectic for Grimes. "There's always an emergency. What I stopped expecting two years ago was that

I'd have a normal day," he laughs. "I come in with a general outline of what I'd like to get done for the day, and then in between deal with all the crap that pops up." Among the pitfalls: impolite tour-takers. "The mansion has so much history to it, it seems like such a shame that we have to worry about people sitting on the furniture," he says. "You can't take off your shoe and kill a bug against that wall, chipping the plaster! Stanford White put that wall there; before he was shot, obviously. The things I've seen!"

Grimes advises performers interested in this type of living history work to make sure their chops are as sharp as can be. "The two skills every actor who works for us needs are improv and improv," he says. "You have to look someone in the eye, and stick with your character through thick and thin. A lot of living history museums hire historians, and we think they've taken the wrong tact, simply because it's easier to teach us actors a whole lot of information and have us regurgitate it at the drop of a hat—that's what we're trained to do. Whereas, a historian would have to learn to act."

Personally, working at the Beechwood has made Grimes a very happy guy. He met his wife, Morgan Balletto, on the job; she performs at the mansion, and is its props mistress. He praises the dedication of his fellow staffers, such as costume designer Louis Seymour, who actually moved to Boston, but continued making highly detailed wardrobes for the mansion. He's extremely satisfied with the high quality of Beechwood's offerings. "We've come so far in respect to the history being imparted in a unique fashion, but remaining accurate," he says proudly—before rushing off to yet another decade in time.

I DREAM OF AFRICA

Lara Kulpa has always been spectacular at multitasking. Not only has she established herself as an actress with roles in film (*Spinning into Butter*), and TV (she was pre-cast on the reality show *The Biggest Loser*), she's won major notice as a plus-size model. Kulpa also created her own very successful Web design and Web marketing firm, and is a volunteer firefighter on Long Island in her spare time. She admits her love for performing drives her tremendously—as does her lifelong passion for zoology, specifically researching the history and behavior of primates.

Kulpa fell into acting and modeling in New York. "Being a plus-size person, I've had a lot of people say to me, 'If you lost weight, you'd be so beautiful.' To which I always say: "Wait a minute! I'm beautiful now,'" she declares. "My friend Tina Dame had been modeling and acting since she was a teenager, and she thought I should be, too. She said, 'You're gorgeous, and you should be doing this, too!' So I talked to her agent, and got some pictures done. I definitely have to thank Tina for dragging me into all that."

How I Got the Spark

At the time that Kulpa was working with TV stars such as Mo'Nique, another dream was burning away inside. "When I was about five years old, I started learning about people who worked with chimpanzees and primates, like Dian Fossey and Jane Goodall," she says. "I always had a love for animals, and I said, you know what? That's what I'm going to do—I knew at five years old. So deep, deep, deep in my heart; my dream was always to be an animal psychiatrist, an animal researcher, go to Africa, climb the mountains, and save the gorillas. This dream is never going to leave me.

"Senior year in high school, I had to do an essay for English class. I decided to do a report on the rainforest, and I thought it would really impress my teacher if I could get an interview with someone who really knew about the subject, so I decided to call up Jack Hanna. I called the Columbus Zoo, asked for his office, and surprisingly, they put me right through. I left a message with his secretary, because he was in Africa at the time, and told her, 'Next time he goes, he has to take me with him!' Then Jack called me back on a Sunday morning at 7:00 AM! My mother comes running down the hall, and wakes me up, and I get on the phone, absolutely flabbergasted. I told him, 'I want to be you! What do I have to do to be you?' He said, 'There's this great school in Gainesville, Florida, the Santa Fe Teaching Zoo, the only one of its kind in the country. If you go there, when you finish, you're a certified zookeeper and animal handler. I recommend you put your application in now.' I said, 'OK!'

"It was the most wonderful program! The classroom itself is built inside the zoo—it was the coolest thing I've ever done. I worked with over eighty-eight species of exotic animals— venomous snakes, antelope, emus. I had to help catch a fourteen-foot alligator who'd escaped her enclosure my senior semester! Mind you, she was missing two limbs, so she couldn't go very far, but somebody had to jump on her, and three or four us did. We picked her up, carried her back to her enclosure, and everything was fine. I loved every minute of it!"

Kulpa has since worked for Lion Country Safari and Neopets, in addition to her modeling and acting work. Melding these two careers may seem daunting, but Kulpa definitely feels up to the challenge. "I always tell people, don't have four million jobs before you're thirty, like I've had!" she admits. "But I've been blessed, because my parents always told me, 'Whatever you want to do, just do it!' "

RELIVING A WONDERFUL LIFE

In the lovely, homespun town of Indiana, Pennsylvania, a truly one-of-a-kind museum experience awaits citizens and visitors alike. The Jimmy Stewart Museum, located on the third floor of the town library, pays tribute to the legendary actor who was Indiana's most famous resident. Stewart's films, photographs, movie props, and personal effects are among the museum's highlights—as is the work of Steve Nevil, creator and performer of *As Always, Jimmy Stewart*, a one-man living history play that brings this great star back to life. When he's not performing at the museum, this veteran performer takes his show on the road—and plays to capacity crowds across the country.

Like many, Nevil first discovered Stewart's work as a young movie fan: "Something about Stewart's naturalism, his way of throwing off a line, of making it seem like what he was saying and doing was actually happening for the first time—this is what inspired me," he recalls. "Watching *Harvey* on TV late one night was truly a transcendent moment for me, and this man became my role model as an actor from then on."

Nevil landed his first "living history" role—playing James Thurber—during his undergrad days at Rio Hondo College in Whittier, California. He further honed his craft at Circle in the Square, and got his first big acting break as a regular on the sitcom *The McLean Stevenson Show*. Steady acting gigs on series such as *Cheers, Lou Grant,* and *The Fresh Prince of Bel Air* followed, but all the while, Nevil's earliest influence was still whispering in his ear.

"I'd always had in the back of my mind the idea of someday doing a show about Jimmy Stewart," he says. "In the late seventies, Stewart was very often seen on *The Tonight Show* with Johnny Carson, telling great tales of old Hollywood, or reading a memorable poem here and there. I took to videotaping these segments with my then brand-new VCR. He was a superb storyteller. For years, I kept these tapes, really not knowing what I would do with them."

The answer came after Nevil was cast in a production of *Spoon River Anthology* at Theatre West in Los Angeles. "After several months of doing the play, I really felt the urge to begin writing something for myself. Part of this was because the essential nature of *Spoon River* deals with various townspeople who come back from the dead to confide the hopes and tragedies of their lives," he explains. "It really got me thinking about how the arc of a particular life, of one person, touches so many other lives." Jimmy Stewart had by this time passed on, and Nevil set out to revive his essence by spending the next eight months crafting three drafts of his tribute, in conjunction with collaborator Ted Snyder.

Nevil plays Stewart as an eighty-six year old, reminiscing about his life and work. "The show takes place in 1994, about six months after the death of Jimmy's wife, Gloria, and he's revealed at the beginning in the den of his Beverly Hills home, where he sequestered himself for the last three years of his life. This play is about loss, about despair, and about how you cope with that feeling on a day-to-day basis. This is a love story about two people who were devoted to each other for forty-five years. Losing someone is inevitable, and hopefully the play shows that grieving, and working through your grief, is a natural process."

Nevil's portrayal of the actor is truly uncanny, and audience reaction has been remarkable. "Mr. Stewart's daughter Kelly came to see the show in 2004—that was truly overwhelming for me," Nevil says. "She wrote me the next day: 'You were wonderful. It is a touching, lovely performance.' " Kelly later sent Nevil a beloved family heirloom as a token of her appreciation—her father's dog-eared script binder, from which he learned his lines. "For me, it was like winning an Oscar," Nevil marvels.

Stewart was a great military hero in addition to being a great actor, and veterans often become quite emotional at performances. "The people who stay behind after the show to talk to me—that is very moving to me," Nevil says gratefully. "For some of the older men who were participants in World War II—some of them bomber pilots like Stewart—it is actually a moment where they seem to be able to open up and talk about those traumatizing events in specific detail."

Tim Harley, executive director/curator of The Jimmy Stewart Museum, first heard about Nevil's work in a cold phone call. "Steve had performed the work both in LA and New York," Harley explains. "He contacted us and very kindly offered us, at his expense, to come and do his show here for a fundraiser." Nevil continues to devote his time to fundraising through his performances for the museum.

Harley is proud that Nevil's work, and the museum, stands as a reminder of the creative and social impact Stewart had on America. "One of the ways we like to hold up Mr. Stewart in the sense of a contemporary role model is, here's a person who very early in his professional career, achieved a great deal of success," he states. "Prior to the beginning of the second World War, he was earning in excess of $200,000 a year. The important thing about Mr. Stewart was—that really didn't change him. His values were so intact. He served in the war and flew over twenty combat missions, and maintained his position in the reserves, retiring as a brigadier general. Also, in very quiet ways, both here in his former community, and in his home on the West Coast, he helped organizations or people that he felt positive about. He was a great supporter of the Los Angeles Zoo; he supported the local fire company here. So our sense in holding him up is: success doesn't necessarily have to change you."

Harley hopes that Nevil's show, plus the energy and attention that supporters like Nick and Nina Clooney (George's mom and dad) and Mr. and Mrs. Rich Little bring to the museum keeps interest in its offerings strong: "The hard material people can learn from here includes our nice collection of his films [Stewart made over eighty during his career], some of which are not readily available elsewhere. We have substantial archives, resource materials that scholars working on aspects of Mr. Stewart's life have available to them."

Nevil hopes interest stays alive in Jimmy Stewart, period. "I have to admit that I'm concerned people may not remember who he was or what he did a few years from now," he says. "But that's part of why I wrote the show—to share the man and reveal the lessons from his life." He intends to do lots more living history performance as well. "There are hundreds of incredible people from history and literature that are just waiting to be presented in a one-person play format!" Stay tuned.

RENAISSANCE MAN

For Douglas Kondziolka, swordplay, bullwhips, and joke telling are all in a day's work. Kondziolka plumbs the past by touring the busy and lucrative US renaissance faire circuit with his partner Jose Granados. They perform the Don Juan and Miguel Show to capacity audiences every autumn. "Don Juan is the Prince of Spain, the great swordfighter and lover," Kondziolka explains. "[My role is] his sidekick, manservant Miguel Rodrigo Jesus Alfredo Esteban de Zaragosa. Don Juan is suave and debonair; Miguel is bumbling, easily duped, and faithful to his master. We have great fun onstage!" Here, Kondziolka discusses his happy life on the road.

Q: How did you get started doing renaissance faires?

A: Jose and I have worked together for nearly thirty years. We met at King Richard's Faire (currently the Bristol Renaissance Faire) near Gurnee, Illinois. I was a madrigal singer in an a cappella group called the Jongleurs, and Jose was a partner in a stage combat group called the Ring of Steel. Jose was already playing Don Juan with the Ring of Steel, and decided the character needed a sidekick. I was hired, and Miguel was born.

We immediately decided that working together was fun, and decided to create our own show. For our first few years, we worked at King Richard's Faires, in Chicago for the summers and outside Boston for the fall. From there, we worked festivals throughout the US. We've done Michigan, Kansas City, Minnesota, Denver, Sarasota, and more. We're currently performing at the Arizona Renaissance Faire, Scarborough Faire, the Renaissance Festival near Dallas, the Sterling Renaissance Faire in New York, the Pennsylvania Renaissance Faire, and the Carolina Renaissance Faire.

Q: Discuss some of the most rewarding aspects of your work.

A: We firmly believe in supporting not only our craft, but also the event where we perform and our fellow entertainers as well. I recall when starting out on the renaissance circuit, more seasoned performers would give me pointers on comedy, timing, movement, and advice regarding the show. Renaissance festivals are, in many ways, a real community, and it is that community support which gives us all success. Plus, I think that success is measured in terms of being able to work at what you love. I'm reminded of a quote by Uta Hagen: "Talent is the ability to work."

What do I love most about my job? So many things, really. I live in an environment of creativity and music. There are so many talented people I get to call friends. I love working with my buddies and pals, and the freedom we have to create our own material. I love the audience—this is not a cliché. I truly honor the people who permit us to do what we love.

Q: What are your proudest accomplishments?

A: We are now creating a production company called Blind Dog Entertainment. With this company we wish to make movies capturing some of the magic of our world. We've produced two films—*Don Juan and Miguel in the Tale of El Gusano*, and our latest, a full-length, award-winning action comedy called *The Lost Princess*, which stars Jose's daughter, Dakota Star Granados, as Princess Esmeralda. Lovely Dakota is twenty years old, has been part of our show for almost ten years—and is a master with a whip! *The Lost Princess* was shown at the 2005 Gloria International Film Festival in Salt Lake City. We wish to continue making films and getting national or international distribution, plus producing CDs through our Blind Dog music label.

two
no business like big business

The corporate world offers a vast array of opportunities for actors seeking job change or expansion. Still, to many performers, getting along with a bunch of suits sounds like a pretty intimidating proposition. Wouldn't working in the business world require learning all about flow charts, number crunching, market research, and other scary-sounding essentials?

Well, it could if you really want to challenge yourself. Two of the actors profiled in this chapter have found great success in the traditional day-to-day office environment. Three others have elected to take on commerce with freelance, free-flow approaches—but they are just as polished and professional as their more corporate counterparts. The major point here: a creative constitution can serve you extremely well in business. Here's food for thought on how you might want to make your personal mark.

A TALE OF TWO TRAINERS

Exec/Comm, a New York City-based executive communications firm, is an industry leader when it comes to helping professionals convey, and stay, on message. Founded by communications pioneer Richard J. McKay in 1982, Exec/Comm works with clients in North America, Europe, Asia, and South America on a variety of business issues, including media management, client relations, negotiation, writing, and presentation, all with a view toward optimum communication strength.

It's really no surprise that such an accomplished corporation would see the value of hiring actors as communication consultants/ corporate trainers. Jim Sterling and Gail Parker both enjoyed very busy performing careers before coming to Exec/Comm, and both found true satisfaction as they translated their acting talents to their new positions—and learned many fascinating new skills at the same time. Here are their stories.

Jim Sterling

Sterling is a full-time consultant with Exec-Comm, plus has a part-time faculty role as well. A dedicated pro, he's been with the company for five years. Sterling averages about a fifty-hour work week; his main duties include phone meetings with clients, teaching, and traveling.

"Performing always seemed to be a part of who I was," he explains. "I did a little acting in high school, and was determined to do much more when I got to college at Dartmouth. And I did—I was in a show virtually every single term. It became a huge part of my life, so I decided to move to New York to act after graduation. Certain things egged me on—I had won an outstanding artist award in college, that got me going, and I thought, I can take on New York, no problem.

"I continued to work pretty much constantly Off-Broadway. I went on summer stock tours a lot of times, and did quite a lot of work through a number of different company memberships, like the Bloomsburg Theatre Ensemble and Jean Cocteau. I also had a small but vital role in the film *Conspiracy Theory* with Mel Gibson."

What made Sterling look elsewhere, career-wise? "I got a day job in an office, and I liked it. It was an administrative assistant in a non-profit. I did some computer work, and interfaced both with my colleagues and our clients; I did very well, got great reviews. So then I was referred to Exec/Comm by a friend of mine who worked here. I pursued the job, and got it, as a faculty member with the company. It was on a part-time basis, which still allowed me to continue my work as an actor."

Even though Jim was working as a trainer at Exec/Comm, he still felt he needed more help finding an additional career direction. "I turned to the Actors' Work Program after I learned about it from one of my fellow faculty members. At that time, I went and got career advice and also connections there," Sterling says. "I credit Actors' Work Program with giving me that lead and opportunity, so I was a faculty member at Exec/Comm AND worked with the New York Health and Hospital Association, doing customer service training for doctors, nurses, and aides. I did both jobs at once for about a year, and it was absolutely a wonderful introduction to the world of training.

"Patch (Schwadron) was really helpful, because I had thought about going for a full-time position with Exec/Comm a lot sooner than I did, and we talked about it, and I came away from that discussion thinking, you know what, it's not the right time yet. I really needed more business experience. My family wasn't really behind it at the time, either. I really didn't reach out for full-time employment for another two years.

"The challenge for me was really gaining that business experience. So what happened was, in addition to being a faculty member, Exec/Comm brought me in for a number of different projects. One was a sales position, and one was a more in-house accounting function. So I was introduced to kind of the nuts-and-bolts of the business. It really expanded my sense of confidence in myself as a business person. I think I really needed to have that in order to go for it, at Exec/Comm, anyway."

What has Sterling specifically overcome in shifting gears? "The biggest challenge I've faced in going into a new career is really, just learning the job. It's like taking on a huge role. You know, where you're kind of intimidated: How am I ever gonna play *King Lear?* How am I ever gonna be a consultant? But I think you come to work every day, and don't try to look at the huge picture, necessarily. My firm is particularly good at setting reasonable goals for performance. So I think if you find yourself meeting those goals, you see you're on the right track."

He also learned that his two career tracks have a fundamental difference: "When I first went into theater, I thought I was going to get a lot of work, because I'm a team player, I work well with people, so they're going to want to hire me again and again. Doesn't work that way." Sterling elaborates, "In theater, you really have to have a real specific idea of who you are in the theater, or in film, or on TV, and be able to find people—casting directors, agents—who want that personality, that type of actor [you are]. You have to be extremely conscious of who you are, and how it profits others. In business, I think you can get away with not necessarily knowing your talents, or knowing who you are, and yet your ability to work well with others can serve you EXTREMELY well."

Sterling's business success has given him a great sense of satisfaction. "Being in front of a group of people, giving a seminar, and really seeing people change their behavior and learn new ways to communicate—teaching—that's definitely the most rewarding part of the job.

"In business, you can achieve goals. You can say, 'OK, we're going to be in front of clients ten times this month.' And there's a goal! And you can achieve it! It's security, and it's also very satisfying to be able to have that accomplishment in your life. Being able to project into the future what you want to do, and then accomplish that, is one of the pleasures of a nine to five existence."

Sterling's words of wisdom for others seeking new work? "My big advice is, go where you are wanted. My friend wanted me to join Exec/Comm, and when I got into Exec/Comm, they kept wanting me. That's the world speaking to you.

"Identifying what you want, and then going after it in a confident way, is very important. I put this quote on my refrigerator: 'Life never hands you anything that you can't handle.' If you have an opportunity, and you really want it, you owe it to yourself to go after it in a nice, strong, confident way, and don't second-guess too much."

Gail Parker

Parker teaches up to two hundred people in a group for Exec/Comm lectures and workshops. She works with the media six days a month, and has a reputation as one of the best in the business.

"At the time I chose to be a theater/communications major at Ithaca College, my father, as well as every wise person I'd ever known, said, 'Don't get a fine arts degree! Get a bachelor of science or liberal arts degree!' But of course, nobody could talk me out of it; I said, 'I'm not doing that.' In hindsight, I think it's wise for an actor to get a liberal arts degree and use all their electives, only because as an actor, the more you know about life, the better off you are.

"I auditioned for the one place I'd wanted to be growing up, the Cleveland Playhouse, in my hometown, and I got in right out of college. I got my Equity card at the ripe old age of nineteen, and experienced rave reviews for my role as Monica in *The Prime of Miss Jean Brodie*. From there, I got relatively cocky, and when I was asked back to the Playhouse, said, 'I'm going to New York.' Another classic error, because I think several years at a rep company is brilliant training.

"So I went to New York at twenty, and got the startling news that EVERYBODY was the star of their hometown, and the competition was tough. The very first thing I auditioned for in New York will always stand out in my mind; it was at the Equity Library Theatre, which no longer exists. It was a terrific showcase, because agents were required as part of their licensing to attend. I walked in, and the stage manager said, 'What are you here for?' I said, 'I'm here to play the lead.' He said, 'Those are agent submissions only. All that's going on here now is a chorus call. But give it a shot if you want to.' So I go, 'OK!'

"That self-confidence lasts a while. You come into an industry where you're told only 2 percent of that industry works at any time, and your attitude had better be, somebody's in that 2 percent! I did have that for a while. I was sent by an agent to a Broadway audition to play a Russian immigrant or something, and the casting director said, 'You're young. On a scale from one to ten, how good an actress are you?' I said, 'Well, I'd love to audition for you so you can see for yourself.' 'The casting director said, 'Thank you anyway.' That was not nice!

"So I decided I'd do children's theater. I went on the road with Barry Weissler's company at that time, a very high-quality company. I worked with the Weisslers very closely for several years, becoming an assistant director, and had very, very positive experiences throughout.

"Through the eighties, I did some national tours. I did the same stock company for eight years in a row, and that's not wise, because you keep going out of town for the whole summer, and all that happens is you get older, and your resume doesn't get any better. Two out of three started to become my rule; director, salary, role you wanna do. It had to be two out of the three, or you had to start saying no, and I didn't learn that early enough. I also didn't learn that brilliant reviews in stock or dinner theater on the road meant nothing to a New York casting director. Agents and casting directors would rather see a showcase review, because they don't know if your aunt the high school English teacher wrote the [road] review for you.

"So I was a working actress, but I wasn't really advancing. I did some nice rep theater, and I had a couple of very good financial years, but there was no real consistency to my career. Also, I liked having more intellectual stimuli in my life.

"I had the great, great, good fortune to work on a couple of Equity committees with Colleen Dewhurst. She would say, 'Good thinking! Gail, you're making a good point.' I would think, 'I'm not supposed to think, I'm supposed to feel!' But when someone that bright, perceptive, and caring takes a second to look you in the eye, you say, 'There's a path for me.'

"The Actors' Work Program had started, and I thought I should think about a parallel career if indeed I wanted more power in my life. I went to the orientation, and Ronda Ormont, who was there at the time, said, 'Let's figure out what you can do.' As an actor, you don't even know your options. But who else can memorize a bunch of lines, bring your own wardrobe to a set, have the director say, all the lines and shots have changed, and then do it? The skills that take are transferable to corporate skills.

"Ronda said to me, 'You walk in the door like a corporate trainer.' I said, 'OK. What's that? I'll try that.' This was the early nineties, and around that time I got married, and my husband did not want me to be on the road. At that point, it was an easier transition for me than for some, because I had my husband, who was more important. That was my choice.

"I was actually sent by the Actors' Work Program first to a wonderful program at Marymount where I learned to be a fitness instructor. It sounds a little off base, but I have a dance, directing, and choreography background. That experience was made to order for corporate training! Corporate training is not about being a diva in the front of the room; it's about, the other person's more important than you are. If you say, how can I help this person be in better

balance with their body, or give a better speech, or be a better nego-
tiator, it really leads to planning a path as you go.

"I was on committees for twelve years at Equity, and was
a counselor at Equity, and it was that credit on my resume that got
me into corporate training. They said, 'You have negotiated; you
have been a businessperson; you have had to think and vote and drive
things forward, and chair national committees. You were elected by
your peers, then reelected.' That what as good as working in a business office to my present firm.

"I changed my 'commercial' at cocktail parties. That was the
first step in Ronda leading me through barriers to change, which is
really hard for an actor. You're giving up your definition of yourself.
When people said, 'What do you do?' to change my answer to 'I'm
a corporate trainer' from 'I'm an actor' was very, very painful. But
I forced myself to go to business networking events, and I met
someone who said, 'I'll train you as a corporate trainer if you help
me schedule some of the training.' I did that for about six months,
met someone who introduced me to Exec/Comm. I started part-
time, they asked me to go full-time, and seven years later, I am in
charge of all training. I'm also director of training and development,
and have brought in lots of actors to work part-time, because they
are the best!

"Ronda said to me back in 1992, 'Do what you like second-best
most of the time.' That's what I'm doing, every single day. I have
benefits, I have a one-woman show to a certain extent, and every day
I get someone saying, 'Thank you!' Do I miss the theater? I miss the
theater a lot. Do I miss the auditioning and the roles I took for
insurance reasons? No!

"I am a human being, I'm not my human doing."

ROLE MODEL

Nicole Bigham has risen to the top ranks of commercial spokesmod-
els by being bright, tenacious, and ultra-professional. Bigham works
for numerous corporations doing advertisements, trade shows, and
live events, and has been on countless magazine covers and interior
spreads.

Bigham's acting skills, honed early through her TV career in
many beauty pageants, have given her the kind of poise that corporate work requires. Bigham also credits her agent, William Ware of

The William Ware Agency in Dallas, as a huge factor in her success (the Ware agency specializes in providing live entertainment performers for events and for corporations such as GTE, VITEK, DCS, Amfac, and many others). Bigham spoke about the lessons she's learned as a model:

"As a child in Pennsylvania, I always watched the Miss America, Miss USA, and Miss Universe on TV—I was always interested in the glamour of pageantry. When I was eleven, my Aunt Marie and Uncle Val asked if I wanted to go to watch my first live pageant—their son, who's a professional ballet dancer, worked with mostly female dancers, some of whom were actually in pageants. I sat in the audience, totally amazed, looking at the beautiful gowns, the hair and makeup, the glitz of it all. I said to my aunt, 'I want to do this; I know I can do this! Can you help me?'

"When we got home from the pageant, my aunt said to my mom, 'I'm sorry, I don't know what I started!' But my mom always said I was the biggest ham, so I think she saw this coming. Mom said, 'If this'll make her happy, let's get her help.' So that's exactly what happened. They got one of the girls who'd been in the pageant to teach me the basics of modeling, got me an evening gown, prepared me to compete. I did my first pageant at twelve; I didn't win, but I went out there, did my best, and loved it. I won my second pageant; once I got that taste of winning, a competitive edge came out in me, and I started doing pageants all the time, sometimes one on a Saturday and another the next day on a Sunday.

"I wanted to win Miss Pennsylvania Teen USA; I'd done it when I was fourteen and fifteen, then won at sixteen—third time's the charm. I went on to the national pageant, Miss Teen USA. I ended up making the top twelve, and even at sixteen, I knew what the magnitude of that was. I also won Miss Pennsylvania USA, and became the second woman to hold both of those titles. Once you're into pageantry, modeling and acting go hand-in-hand. Once you start to network, it's like you're on a tree branch that's growing out. I just started climbing the ladder, starting to model, getting into acting. By no means has it been an easy road, but my mom Judith Ann has always been a great networker, too, to help me. She's a pistol, let me tell ya! She was never a stage mom, but helped and encouraged me however I asked her to.

"I knew I had something special when I entered the famous modeling agent John Casablancas's Great American Model Search, and I won. When they called my name, I just stood there, because I couldn't believe it. It was huge. There were two hundred contestants, and I thought, I'll do OK, but at that time, I had clear braces. But then after I won, and the shock wore off, I thought, OK, I can do this. I have something that I can make money with. I was fifteen, sixteen.

"It was a big deal when I got my first national ad for GNC (General Nutrition Centers)—my picture was all over the country. Being on two dozen billboards throughout the Pittsburgh area—I'd drive down the road and see myself, and wave at me! It's was just so exhilarating, friends would call me up and say, 'Girl, I just saw you on freakin' Route 51!' It was hysterical. I started doing so many commercials and ads. When I got my first cover, which was *Whirl Magazine*, it was amazing to walk over to the newsstand and see myself. I've done so many calendars and posters that are in circulation all over the world. For different magazine shoots, I've been a bride so many times—and I've never been married! You know, if you don't have many, many accomplishments in the modeling industry, that means you're not doing too well. If you're not continuously updating your portfolio, you're not doing the right thing career-wise, and I update mine all the time.

"To be successful, number one, you need a good agency. You need an agency that believes in you, because those people get you the work. Work ethic is so important. Most people think this is such a glamorous life, that they do your hair and make-up and you go recite your lines or whatever. It's not like that at all; having a good work ethic means showing up on time, communicating, being professional with the people you work with. You have to have positive attitude and a great personality, because if you don't, trust me, word travels. I know this first hand, because I'm also a model manager now, and if I hear that a girl is always late or always wanting to take breaks, or doesn't look prepared, I don't want to work with this person.

"It's all about who you know in this industry. Don't get me wrong, talent's gonna get you far, but it's all about who you know. Somebody could call you up and be like, 'I've got this gig, it's real small, it only pays $200 a day.' But you could network, and you never know who you might meet. So I try never to pass something like that up. I'll work for two months straight. I have business cards with my picture on them, a half-body shot and a full-body shot.

Once people know you won't show up intoxicated or on drugs, you will have work. People will call you.

"I'm twenty-nine years old. In this business, I should be over already. But I'm working more than I ever have in my entire life, and it's because of my work ethic, because I've been able to network, have good presentation, whether it's print, commercial, runway, or promotion. Once you have a good name out there, people will want to use you.

"Have a good head on your shoulders. Show that you're not afraid to work—if I have to work an eleven-hour day, I work an eleven-hour day. The money that we make in this industry is at times ridiculous when you consider there are people out there working nine to five, making minimum wage. We can make $500 or more a day. Once I made a comment about ONLY making a large amount of money on a certain job, and my mom and aunt looked at me incredulously. My mom said, 'Nicole, do you know your little cousin has to work two weeks to get what you're making in a day?' Wow, did that slap me in the face! So I always try to keep myself very level headed—these are blessings I've been given. I've got to use them wisely, because somebody out there's busting her ass to make $6.25. If I'm a model manager at an event and a girl's bitching, I always give her that perspective.

"A lot of time, if people see you as an actor, they don't know whether you're sincere. For me, I think my acting skills have helped me communicate with people, though. It's so much easier to approach people; you're more comfortable with yourself, and self-confident. If someone says, 'You need to come up here and give a speech', there's no stage fright. I'm able to talk to a brick wall if I have to.

"I get to experience so much, from being at the Super Bowl, sitting in the New England Patriots' end zone, and getting a tour of the grounds, or doing a job on a Caribbean island. I don't know where this is going to lead me, who knows?

"The job I'm doing right now is promoting US Smokeless Tobacco. They hire four models to be on site and promote the product. The man I'm with, Matt, does promotion for Captain Morgan liquor. We met on a job in the Caribbean—that's another plus to this job, you might meet your significant other! It's so wonderful, because we're in the same industry, and we understand each other's work.

"I'd love to act in movies or TV, but my education is in broadcasting and communications, so I'd love to be an entertainment broadcaster. I like interviewing people—to go to the Oscars and be on the red carpet, I'd love to do something like that. I've also thought about owning my own company, in image consulting. Because of my history, I think I'd be very good at something like that. I could work in fashion or make-up. There are so many possibilities, but right now, I'm continuing to work at modeling.

"Am I proud of all of my accomplishments? Absolutely! All of these accomplishments are so important, because they've contributed to my forward motion. I'm still going, and I'll let you know when I'm satisfied."

THE QUICK STUDY

Amanda Melby can do so many things so well. Splitting her professional time between Phoenix and Los Angeles, Melby has a long list of film and TV jobs under her belt, is a noted cellist, teaches private classes in acting, music, and exercise, works for the Phoenix Film Project, works on *Screen Wars*, a TV show she hosts, does film and TV jobs, and is a wife and new mom, too!

A staple of Melby's business is corporate product demonstration. She works monthly in the commercial business world of product demonstration at trade shows, conventions, and events. The work requires sharp concentration, top-notch communication skills, and big-time flexibility, and this is how she got to the top of the field.

School, and the School of Life

"I went to Concordia College on a music scholarship for cello, and declared a double major in music and theater. Both required huge amounts of work outside the classroom, and I wasn't able to maintain both majors and still graduate on time. I changed my music major to English, kept my theater major, and continued playing cello in the orchestra and in private lessons.

"After graduation, I was unsure if I wanted to pursue acting or arts management. Fortunately, I had received a prestigious arts management internship from the Kennedy Center in Washington, DC, so my decision was made for me for the time being. After a few years of living and working in arts management, I realized I was starving myself. I was watching others perform and be artists, but the demands of my job didn't allow me to be an artist myself.

"About the same time I was making this personal revelation, the non-profit I was working for in Cleveland was in financial trouble, and I was laid off. What a blessing in disguise! It allowed me to get my acting game back in gear. I got an agent, got cast in a play, and started working. I was very fortunate that Cleveland had a busy market. I worked in theater, film, commercials, industrials, voice-overs, and print. I actually made a living doing this, and was fortunate to be able to join AFTRA, SAG, and AEA, all while living and working in Cleveland.

"After a few years, I headed out to LA and hoped for bigger jobs. What I found was steady, small project work and a reunited passion for my craft. I was accepted into Howard Fine's master class, and loved the challenge of putting up quality work every week. I cherish the time at his studio. It was there that I really defined my own process of creating a character and working. Howard and Heidi Helen Davis, my other coach there, were extremely influential in my development."

Showing Things to the Best Advantage

"I don't really see product demonstration as acting, but there are certain skills I use from my acting training, and certain things I can learn from product demonstration (to use) in my acting. For example: improv. When I work as a product specialist, there is generally no script. I have the facts, but I can craft them into the presentation whatever way I see best. We are taught to analyze the crowd and tailor the presentation to the crowd. Many times, even though I am on a raised platform with a microphone, people will still feel that it's OK to come up to the platform, or ask a question in the middle of a sentence. These situations definitely force me to be a quick thinker, and react appropriately to the situation.

"My preparation is also different. For any commercial work or product specialist work, the prep work is more about the facts and the brand. For roles in film and theater, the prep work is more about the feelings and the person; I do a character bio and back story, and really look at the objectives, motivation, and actions of the character."

Job Wisdom

"I realized long ago I shouldn't try to ace auditions, because inevitably, when I feel like I've aced it, I don't book it. I think commercial auditions taught me that lesson the best. Sometimes it's not about how good or talented you are, it's that you don't look like the girl in the storyboard. Or you look too much like the director's ex-girlfriend. Or your look wouldn't work with someone they've already cast. Too many things are out of my hands to control the hiring process. What I am sure to do is be prepared. To do my homework; to present myself as a professional. And if all factors are in alignment, I'd be grateful that I booked the job."

Why I'm Happy

"I don't think success is becoming a household name or earning a certain dollar amount. For a few years, I didn't do anything artistic whatsoever. I worked in a cubicle. When I was able to free myself from those confines and really blossom as an artist, I felt success. I work every day as an artist. That is success."

three
the body electric

Physicality—use it correctly, and it sets you free as a person. Actors are especially in tune with their bodies and minds, using both as primary instruments. This type of consciousness is extremely rare among the general population, however—so actors who want to help others feel physically and mentally better have a huge range of ways in which to make important societal impact.

In this chapter, we're going to meet four people who've used their knowledge of the body and mind to make other people's lives better. There's the glamorous celebrity who's now made the empowerment of women her primary focus; the caring medical professional; the smart actor whose sideline success helps others de-stress; and the kindly human services worker who risks danger in order to aid kids in emotional crisis. All four deserve the utmost in praise for their efforts.

FEMINISM, FREEDOM, AND FITNESS

Sheila Kelley has earned countless fans and critical accolades for the emotionally luminous characters she's created. Kelley's talent lit up movies like Cameron Crowe's *Singles*, Ridley Scott's *Matchstick Men*, and Neil LaBute's *Nurse Betty*, plus television shows such as *LA Law*, *Sisters*, and *ER*. It's her current work as founder of the fitness movement Sheila Kelley's S Factor, however, that allows her to make the impact on others she feels is most worthwhile.

In 2000, while producing and starring in the film *Dancing at the Blue Iguana*, Kelley discovered the provocative and beautiful art of striptease. She perfected her talents at this physical craft, and incorporated it into a fully-developed workout for women. After she began giving classes to enthusiastic friends such as Teri Hatcher, Sheila Kelley's S Factor simply exploded.

Kelley now runs a 5,000-foot studio in Los Angeles, a great second space in San Francisco, and is about to conquer New York City as well. She authored the book *The S Factor: Strip Workouts for Every Woman*, has taught over 4,000 students, and produced three top-selling fitness DVDs. She's happily wed to actor Richard Schiff of TV's *The West Wing*, and has two kids she adores. So what's left for her to achieve? Spreading her message of emotional empowerment through exercise even further! Here, she starts by discussing the process of accessing emotions through her creative work:

"I think there were moments in the films *Singles* and *Breaking In* that were just cathartic moments—life can unfold in front of the camera. There's an ongoing argument about whether acting is interpretive art, or creative art. It's a very interesting argument, because you're creating the emotions, but you're also saying words that are interpreted. It's a bilingual art form. I think the moments that most struck me were when I found the creative art form of acting outweighed and outshone the interpretive parts. Those organic, truthful moments created out of nothing—not written, but coming from you creatively. It's like emotional art. I think one of those moments was the scene where my character Debbie Hunt in *Singles* is doing a video date, 'Welcome to Debbie Country.' That was totally improv, and totally created by me, and we were just riffing the whole day—that was the moment that the character became purely connected to me, emotionally, physically, and psychologically. It's one of those moments you can't forget, that you created out of nothing.

"At the age of about thirty, I had one kid; Richard and I were together. I'm doing auditions that I think are mind-blowing, awesome, incredible, cathartic—and not getting the jobs. I'm sitting there going, 'Bummer, bummer, I'm depressed, my life sucks.' I picked up the book *David Copperfield*, I read the first line—and my life changed. Boom! Like that. The first line is, "Whether I turn out to be the hero of my own life, or whether that station will be occupied by another, these pages must show.' It blew my life open! All of sudden, I went, 'I am not being my own hero! I'm waiting for somebody else to do it. I'm waiting for somebody else to hire me, to write the right role, to get the talent that I know I have.'

"That's when I decided to produce *Dancing at the Blue Iguana*. I decided that I was going to hire the director, find the money—and it unfolded exactly like that, when I became my own hero. It was a huge moment for me so every step I take in life now is predicated on that line. I don't want to end up an old woman, looking back on my life, with any regrets about not having made anything happen.

"So that quote made the movie happen, and the movie made me fall in love with pole dancing, and led [to the idea of] S Factor, which is organic feminine movement. I finished the film, found out I was two months pregnant, had the baby, felt horrible and yucky and fat and milk-cowy, as everyone does. I missed that very cocky, young, alive, light-on-her-feet sexy woman that I had become. So I put a pole in my house, and everything changed from that day forward. I just lived truthfully and organically what my love and my bliss were, whether people thought I was a freak or not. And many people did—they went, 'What, are you crazy?' This was way back, before the whole revolution I've started. Having a pole in your house was just not done. Things are too puritanical—we live in too much fear in this country.

"I didn't care, because I know how beautiful I felt, and I know I'm a good person, and I know I have a lot of morals, values, and ethics. If I loved doing this, if it made me feel powerful and beautiful, that's all I needed. If I could expose my children to the purity of the female body, and [teach them] not to be afraid of the beauty and the power that lives within a woman's body, I've given something to the world.

"It's been an extraordinary journey, and one that I treasure immensely. Every day, I get moved emotionally, profoundly, and deeply by the women who come to my studio to take class with me or any of my twenty-five teachers here. It's frightening for women, because women aren't used to living at 100 percent of their bodies. They're used to living with a little bit of shame in their shoulders, and a little bit of fear in their pelvises, and they don't move it. Everything gets locked up, because God forbid, if they actually lived in their bodies, proudly, with no shame, and with no apology, what could happen?

"Because (at the time of this interview) October is coming up, I'm writing a global newsletter (found on the Sheila Kelley's S Factor Web site) about witchy women. Kind of something fun. But as I've explored the Salem Witch Hunts, it was brutal what happened to women. It's brutal what society can do, and how over the course of hundreds of years, society has turned a woman's body into something that's vilified when it's appropriate, and how it's worshiped when it's appropriate, as seen from a male point of view. What we're missing in the world is looking at the world from a female point of view. That's what I'm trying to give people.

"The roots [of this oppression] go back to the fall of the Pagan religion, the rise of Christianity and patriarchal society, to the fall of a partnership society. I've done a lot of research on this, and I can talk a blue streak about where we women went right, where we went wrong. It's been an extraordinary journey for women, and I really feel that S Factor is not just a great physical workout, but a great political movement. It's going to change the temperature of the world. Think about it: every war's been fought over a woman's body.

"I'm trying to tell people that yes, you can move your body this way, and swing around a pole, and it cannot be for a man. It can be for you. From my point of view, I don't find any of my students erotic, that doesn't turn me on, I don't swing that way. But I find it beautiful and powerful, and men find it erotic and sexual. There are two points of view, and I think if I've given anything through S Factor to the world, it's that knowledge.

The letters I get from women, the e-mails I get, the phone calls, the smiles I get in class, the tears, the laughter—it feeds every ounce of me. I was born a warrior for women. Since I was three, I've felt the inequity. I've been able to see that the emperor has no clothes. You're telling me that you (men) can have naked women writhing around a pole that you guys get to go to and you can throw a dollar at her crotch, and that's OK? And a normal woman doesn't learn to do that because why—she'll be a whore, and she won't be your Madonna-wife?

"When I see a woman in class feeling herself as a whole, a sublime look comes over her face—it's a revelatory moment. It's pure surrender to your body—you've let your brain go, you're in safe hands, and you just surrender to your body's natural, organic, exaggerated movement. These women turn into stunningly gorgeous, liquid moving bodies. It's just incredible. When you know you've affected someone's life profoundly, you can't ask for more in life, you know? You're really DOING something.

"There's about twenty-five of us—three in San Francisco, a bunch here in LA, and we're training more for New York. It's hard to stay in touch—I wish I could have a teachers' class and meeting every week. But hopefully, having studied with me, it lives in them. They study with S Factor for over a year. We're beginning to experiment, because we're growing so fast, we have to bring out teachers quicker. I will look for potential in a teacher, and it's an indefinable thing you look for, because I call my teachers 'body whisperers.' It's way of looking into someone's body—not into the psyche, not into the emotions, but helping someone's body speak. It's an extraordinary talent, and it's rare. If teachers have a touch of it, they can develop it further. In the S Factor studio, when you're around women all day, in this incredibly supportive, loving, empowering environment, you begin to almost be able to read these women's minds innately. It's that sixth sense women have.

"Right now, we're in a hyper-growth stage. Keeping that in mind, I have two children and an extraordinary husband who I'm mad for. We've been together seventeen years, and we're like teenagers. I'm so crazy about him. It's been very hard, actually, with the amount of time this studio and company demands, but my children, husband, and family are my priorities. They feed me, so that I can feed everyone who comes in here. It's a very delicate balance.

"I am a radical feminist—who's in love with men!"

COMFORT AND JOY

The alarm clock blares at 4:00 AM, and it's time for Dennis Rees to start another long day. He does some yoga, then goes for a thirty-to forty-minute run. Then he puts in a couple of hours of studying till his classes at Bergen Community College in New Jersey start at 8:00 AM. He's in class deep into the afternoon, then rushes home, cramming in more study time while his four-year-old daughter Chloe naps. Then it's on to chores like dealing with dinner and scrubbing dishes in the evening. He studies even more, then falls into bed at 9:00 or 10:00 PM. Two days out of the week, he's doing clinical at a local hospital. Such is the nursing life.

Although he still does occasional industry work like stand-in stuff, Rees is now firmly on a medical career track. Here's how he came to make the switch from acting to nursing, starting with the history of his creative work:

"Derek Jacobi's *Hamlet* was basically my lifeblood. I was raised on him. I was born and raised in Los Angeles, so I got to, at the Olympic Arts Festival in 1984, do both Cyrano and Benedict. I saw him a few times, and his work had a profound effect on me.

"I excelled at acting, dance, fencing, all those fun things. I did a teenage drama workshop at California State University, Northridge, which has a very good drama department, and I went to college there as well. At the same time I was in college, I was also doing ninety-nine-seat Equity waiver theater in Hollywood, with people from TV and film trying to gets their onstage chops, while I was trying to get a springboard into TV and film! It was actually kind of fun. You'd be onstage in a Shakespeare doing *King John* with a couple of the daughters from *Eight Is Enough*.

"Then I did about thirteen years of rotating classical rep in the western region of the country. I've been in most of Shakespeare's plays; some productions were pretty good, some of them bad, a lot of it overproduced stuff that was just filling a slot in a commercial season, which is unfortunate. I wasn't really satisfied with the training at Northridge, so I went to the League of Professional Actor Training Programs, and ended up crashing an audition for Carnegie Mellon University, a school I'd never even heard of. I got into Carnegie, graduated in 1989. My final three summers there, I was also at the Utah Shakespeare Festival. It was a pivotal event, well-respected, hard-core classical rotating rep. You worked hard, but it was amazing.

"I was always the bridesmaid, never the bride—not quite true, I had some success. We also used to say how narrow casting people's perspective was for TV and film, but it's also true for stage. One of my little mottos was 'I'm neither fish nor fowl.' I could play the leading guys, and also play the character guys. I knew I could play a little of both types, but that was kind of difficult for the casting people to understand.

"I auditioned for the Ashland Shakespeare Festival in 1984, and six years later made it happen. It was a phenomenal gig, and it lasted about four years, a real career highlight. I played Henry XI in a beautifully truncated version of the trilogy. I always tell people that I don't mourn my career transition, because artistically, I feel I could die happily—I feel very blessed by the wonderful experiences I've had. I've been onstage in some of the best recreations of Elizabethan theatres in the country.

"From Ashland I went to San Francisco, and got to perform in more modern musicals than I'd ever done before. At San Jose Civic Light Opera, I played Perchik in *Fiddler on the Roof*, and Pedro the whip-cracker in *Man of La Mancha*. I won a Dramalogue award for *Into the Woods* at TheaterWorks in Palo Alto. One of my most gratifying experiences was performing opposite my wife, Charlene Tosca Rees, in *Cat on a Hot Tin Roof* at Fleetwood Stage in New Rochelle, New York. I did some TV, *Law & Order: Criminal Intent*, and film, including *Kate & Leopold*. Again, that theme of less and less logic to casting and getting a role kept coming up, though. When I sensed it happening, I didn't get bitter about it. I thought, you either adapt, or you change, or you die. I just thought, why do this to myself? Things just weren't as fun. I always thought, sales suck— whether you're trying to sell Maseratis, or pens, or yourself as an actor in the business. I looked at myself as a thoroughbred in theater, only preoccupied with the art. And that doesn't work.

"One of the themes for me in life has been goals. When I have not had goals, that's when I've really gone adrift. Right before my career change, I had really gone without a goal for some time. On many occasions, when the acting was drying up, I was drawn to the idea of a regular job—it was very seductive. At the same time, there was the fear of detachment of your life as an actor. But it doesn't have to be that way. Life is all about change. The most invigorating moments come with change.

"Economic factors also became a problem. [To maintain] SAG insurance, you had to make about twice as much as you did three years before. It just wasn't fun pounding the pavement. The gap between artistic moments in my life was getting wider and wider— I was getting just as much satisfaction from reading a Shakespeare play to my young daughter Chloe as acting would give me.

"I became very excited at the prospect of becoming knowledgeable about something solid. I wanted to learn some tools to take care of my daughter and wife, not just myself, as the world is becoming a stranger and stranger place. So I found a profession, nursing, for which there is a great demand. There's a saying that in nursing, if you get bored, it's your own fault. There are unlimited possibilities, so many avenues to pursue. It's people-oriented, which I was drawn to.

And interestingly, it is such a diametric opposite to the ethereal intangibles of theater. It's blood and guts and bodily fluids, and yet rooted in humanity.

"I went to the Actors' Work Program to explore how it could help me realize the career I had already mapped out. Patch was wonderful; I wound up receiving a generous scholarship from the program. I found a well-respected training program at Bergen College in Paramus, New Jersey, that would cost me relatively little money and provide me with a low-level degree to get my foot in the door to receive my RN license. That was my game plan. I had conferred with nursing recruiters and hospital nursing boards, and they all agreed that this path was perfect for me. It's a two-year associate degree. The beauty of an RN license is that you can get it whether you're at an associate, bachelors, or masters level.

"Nursing is a constant process of maneuvering around personalities. Obviously, you're dealing with extreme situations, and the best and the worst come out of people, whether you're the sick or the person taking care of the sick. All of the sense work, dance, movement, and communication skills I've had I use in nursing—awareness, sensitivity to emotions. A sense of humor comes in handy, as does a decent singing voice. You never know when you're going to want to soothe someone. There are little moments of humanity you can bring to the job. We had a man who'd been on a ventilator, and he was in a very dark room. I asked the nurse who was there with him, 'Do you mind if I open the shades and let a little light in?' This person was lying like a mushroom in this very dark room. Couldn't we at least give him a little light? The nurse there hadn't thought of that.

"You achieve a certain level of comfort in a career spanning twenty-eight years, as I did with acting. A career change can knock you down, pummel your ego. But I try to take thoughts of humiliation and terror in the hospital clinical setting and turn them around, make them learning experiences, turn them into positive things. I'm not a great test taker, so I started calling the first test I'd have to take in a class 'the first date.' It's the first time you get to know a teacher, and how that teacher's going to question you. So I would dress up in a suit or tie, as opposed to my grungy workout clothes. And I'd do pretty well on the test! And it became quite contagious—other people in my class would dress up a little bit, too. I said, 'By the end of the semester, I want to see us all in formalwear.'

"I've got no health background whatsoever, and a lot of the students around me do. It put me at somewhat of a disadvantage. I've had to go from zero to one hundred as far as my vocabulary is concerned. I really had no basis, so I have a pocket dictionary, take it everywhere, and look up everything. You have to be a sponge.

"When people tell me, 'Wow, it's so amazing, what you're doing' (changing careers), I always tell them about the single mothers I know who are attempting to care for children while working full-time and going to nursing school. It's inspiring and so touching when you look at what they go through, and makes you take inventory. It's that cliché, but if they can do it, I can, too. Older folks going back to school—in these socio-economic times, that's very inspiring, too. I keep perspective looking at the students around me.

"At this point, I'm looking at an internship somewhere like Columbia. My altruistic fantasy goal would be to help somewhere like an Indian reservation.

"Career change is considered one of the most profound psychological stressors in life. But actors are ideally suited for change. Throw yourself into it as you would a role, play it like a role if you must—but let go of the fear."

BREATHE AND BE FREE

Brian Carpenter's acting talents have earned him roles in Woody Allen's *Manhattan*; on TV shows like *Saturday Night Live, Murder, She Wrote*, and *The Practice*; and onstage interpreting the work of Amy and David Sedaris, among other great playwrights. He's primarily a successful actor in Los Angeles, but has found lucrative supplementary work as a massage therapist as well. Carpenter finds a lot of his acting skills can actually be applied to give his massage clients a better quality of life. Here, he talks about both sides of his work life.

"I grew up in Brownsville, Texas, which is on the Mexican border, so there wasn't a whole lot of interest in English-speaking theater. Most of the people in Brownsville spoke Spanish as a first language. So instead of doing plays in junior high school and high school, I ended up doing poetry interpretation competitions, which I could do by myself, as opposed to being in a cast. I placed third in the state of Texas during my junior years of high school. That sort of gave me my fix. Also, it gave me a real education in verse.

"At Harvard my freshman year, I did what's called a house play, as the various houses put on extracurricular plays. I played opposite Lindsay Crouse. I didn't know who she was at the time, she was just some freshman girl, but years later, after I'd become an actor, I saw a rerun of Edward R. Murrow's program. He was interviewing Lindsay and her father, Russell Crouse, the theater writer/composer, and her mother, and I learned his partner was named Lindsay. Lindsay's full name is Lindsay Ann Crouse—like 'Lindsay and Crouse.' So then it all made sense! Anyway, I was in this play, but as result of being in the play, turned in a paper late, got my grade lowered by a full letter, and missed the dean's list. That was the end of my extracurricular involvement, as I decided I should probably pay attention to my studies.

"I went back to Texas to go to law school. At the end of the first year, my class put on a talent show in which we skewered our life at law school. I had a few small parts in a few skits, but ended up spending more time on the talent show than in any of my classes. Should have been a big clue to me then! We put on the show, and it was a riotous success. After the show, the cast and crew had a good old-fashioned drinking party to celebrate. As the evening progressed, someone had the bright idea to encourage everyone to get up on a coffee table and give a drunken reprise of their performances. One act after another got up on the coffee table and entertained the troops. I didn't really have a scene to do, but a friend of mine said, 'Brian, get up there and do some Shakespeare for us!' So I found myself up on this coffee table, everyone was hooting and hollering, and I began Prospero's speech from *The Tempest*. I was one with the material and the audience—everyone was all ears. I finished the monologue, and everyone clapped and cheered and laughed. On the way out, people said, 'You've missed your calling, Brian.' I thought, maybe I have missed my calling.

"The final straw for law school was when I was in the hospital during finals my senior year and I thought, you know what, maybe this is a sign. I dropped out after three semesters and switched to a masters in speech, which I got at the University of Texas. I did *Yankee Doodle: A Bicentennial Musical Revue* in 1976, a bus-and-truck show that toured Texas. I moved to New York in 1977. It was a great place to learn to be a professional. I learned you had to be organized, you had to keep your appointments, you had to say what you wanted from someone in about fifteen seconds when you called them or they'd hang up on you.

"I was in a play in 1978 called *Panhandle* with Bruce Willis. That was way before he was famous, even before he was a bartender at Cafe Central. All the casting directors in New York came to see the play because they were looking at the lead guy, this tall blonde model, and overlooked both Bruce AND me. That's the way it goes sometimes.

For the ten years I lived in New York, I didn't do anything except acting, with a little unemployment insurance thrown in on the side. One of the reasons for this was that I did a lot of extra work in New York City. I could also do print work—I had a Midwestern look that was very appealing to Madison Avenue. I also discovered I had great hands, so I could do hand modeling. Some models said they had excellent hands, so I said, you know what, I'm gonna say I have excellent hands. As a part of a job, they had me hold up a product box, so I had hand pictures, and had cards made up of my hands. My hands were in the opening credits of the movie *The Fan*, and in a very famous Snickers commercial—I did about a hundred hand commercials. There were many ways I could make a living.

"When I got to California, though, I discovered the Screen Extras Guild; there was a class of people who did the extra work. That was what they aspired to, that was their career, and in California, there was a long-standing notion that there was a difference between actors and extras. You don't want to be known as an extra in California if you want to be an actor. There is still this lingering prejudice. Hand modeling was technically extra work as well. Print work was $150 an hour in 1987; it's still $150 an hour as of 2005. So the things that I relied on to make money in New York were simply not available. So I started doing game shows—I won a lot of money. I was on *The $20,000 Pyramid, Scrabble, Greed, Hollywood Squares*. I was the three-day undefeated champ on *Wheel of Fortune*, and I won $30,000.

"I've done massage therapy now for eleven and a half years. I do four to six massages a week. I've discovered that if I tell someone I'm an actor, they're sort of remotely interested in that, especially in Los Angeles, but if I tell someone I'm a massage therapist, they're immediately very interested, because I could touch them, and move them, and maybe improve their life. But acting is sort of in the ether somewhere.

Massage therapy, I've learned, is a wonderful complement to acting, because it's not about me. It's not about how cute I am, it's about taking care of another human being, and helping them. It took me a few years of doing it to realize there are great connections between what I've learned as an actor, and how I can be an effective massage therapist. I know from acting exercises that if you relax completely, breathe slowly and deeply, and allow a little bit of sound to come out with your breath a lot of emotions can come out with that as well. We store a lot of stress in our bodies. Relaxation and breathing is not original thinking, it's been around for a long time, but it's amazing how many people are out of touch with their bodies. You have to be aware that you're tensing up, then give yourself permission to relax.

"It's great, because not only am I helping someone in the hour that I'm working with them, I'm giving them a tool they can use when they're in a traffic jam and the old adrenaline is pumping. Some people don't get it, but the first thing you learn as a massage therapist is that everyone is wired differently, and some people are just gonna be tense. But other people really take it to heart, and it seems to really improve their lives, and I love that.

"I've always considered myself a Romantic with a capital *R*. Going to Harvard! Hitchhiking across Europe! Being an actor! I've had great experiences, like working opposite Mel Gibson on *We Were Soldiers*. I had less than twelve hours' notice. They called me up at eight o'clock one night, said we want you on set at 7:00 AM, you're working with him. I had a great day! It was a wonderful experience, not only working with Mel Gibson from whom I learned a great deal, but working with Randall Wallace, who's a wonderful, kind director, and who played with me. I just loved it! The scene was cut from the theatrical version of the film, but it's on the DVD.

"I've pursued things because I could, and I wanted to. I enjoy the work, I feel I'm good at the work, and it continues to challenge and motivate me."

SOUL SURVIVAL

Megan Cole is gifted with the kind of rare acting talent that both entertains and profoundly enlightens. Cole, a veteran actress with credits ranging from *Seinfeld* to *ER*, has long been lauded for her stage work (she's won three Los Angeles Drama Critics' Awards). In 1995, she originated the groundbreaking role of cancer patient Vivian Bearing in *Wit*, Maragret Edson's eloquent Pulitzer Prize–winning stage play, at South Coast Repertory. As she performed to capacity crowds, Cole discussed the piece with scores of audience members, and was deeply affected by the personal experiences they related. Cole's character, an unemotional college professor who reclaims her life force while facing death in *Wit*, deals with cold, indifferent doctors during her illness; many people described going through the same difficulty in real life.

Cole decided to take action against this disturbing problem; the result became a highly respected doctor-training course, "The Craft of Empathy," which she designed and teaches at medical schools across the country. A Phi Beta Kappa graduate of Lawrence University, Cole is now an artist-in-residence at the University of Texas's Houston Health Center. She's worked with doctors and doctors-in-training at such prestigious institutions as Johns Hopkins and Columbia University's College of Physicians, and is widely praised by the medical community for her innovative performance/teaching techniques.

Emotional intelligence has always been one of Cole's strong suits. "I was a painfully shy child with a bad stutter and wonderful but emotionally unavailable parents," she recalls. "I had been playing the flute and the piano from a very early age, and loved the attention I got from performing. I felt curiously safe onstage, behind my flute, as it were, or behind the piano. So when I wandered into the theater department at Lawrence University, I felt at home, both onstage and behind the mask of a character. I could be both me and not me. And since a character was patently NOT me, I could safely invest a whole lot of me in a performance."

As her professional career progressed to include her role in *Wit*, Cole had an unexpected epiphany. "After performances of *Wit*, audience members would frequently come to me, in person or by mail, to say how much the play had meant to them," she says. " 'I feel as if I'm able to mourn my grandmother for the first time,' one woman said. 'My wife died of cancer six months ago,' a young man wrote, 'and in some way I don't understand, the play is helping me accept her loss.' 'God, this is EXACTLY my experience,' exclaimed many cancer survivors. 'I'm so glad to be given a voice.'

"But what I repeatedly noted was that many doctors who saw the play had a very different reaction. 'Well,' they'd say, 'it's a fine play, but you know, the reality of the doctor/patient relationship is nothing like that.' And that disparity of perception between patients and physicians led me to wonder if there might be something from my acting knowledge that might be useful in narrowing that gap."

Cole's skill set as an actress was put to immediate and effective use when she decided to turn her attention to creating an academic program with which to tackle this issue. "In my course, 'The Craft of Empathy' (which is variously titled 'Developing the Skills of Conscious Equanimity' and 'Balancing Engagement and Attachment'), I draw on actors' skills for being both inside and outside a character at the same moment," she explains. "One of the things I hear most often from doctors is the fear that if they become too emotionally involved with their patients, they risk losing their professional objectivity. What I try to suggest is that when we make conscious choices about our behavior and have techniques for balancing our involvement and non-involvement (which is, of course, what actors do) the fear of losing the Self in the Other is greatly diminished, because we are in control at all times."

Regarding course specifics, "The skills I focus on include identifying the inner witness; using conscious breathing; behaving 'as if'; analyzing through action/objective/obstacle; considering the role of status; and being aware of subtext and nonverbal signals, as well as given circumstances, both in ourselves and in others," Cole imparts. "The principles [of the course] include balance, equanimity, awareness, choice, empathy, compartmentalizing, perspective, self-monitoring, focus, and intention."

Cole's teaching method is hands-on. "Each class is a combination of my talking about and demonstrating these principles and skills, along with some interactive exercises and group discussion," Cole says. "I try to avoid being too didactic or academic, and focus instead on a BALANCE of emotional engagement and intellectual detachment, so that the class itself is a model of the subject matter."

As Cole teaches the course to an increasing number of students, she never loses sight of the fact that she, too, is continually learning new emotional truths. "The most important lesson that the medical students consistently teach me is to remember that each person's perspective is different and equally valid, and that none of us has a patent on the truth," she stresses. "This is a point that I in fact teach, but that I re-learn every time I say something that seems slam-dunk obvious to me, and I'm challenged by a student whose point of view is different from mine. Revisiting humility is always a good thing."

BRAVE HEART

Leanna Foglia's made her mark onstage, in movies—and on the lives of countless kids facing the darkest moments in their lives. As a specialist in crisis management working the toughest streets in Baltimore, Foglia makes a difference in families' lives on a daily basis. Here she talks about how the creative work she's done as an actress has played a part in her life, and her vital work.

"After graduating from high school, I knew I had a strong interest in human services—therapy, psychology. Growing up in a large, blended family, I'd learned so much about people and relationships. But I also had a strong interest in performing, and had done it forever. I had to really sit down with my parents and decide what to pursue. My mother said, 'I would very much prefer that you go with something more concrete, and then pursue your interest in acting on the side.' I agreed—I didn't feel too much of a loss, because I figured the arts would always be a part of my life. So I went to Carnell College in Pittsburgh, and dual-majored in biology and psychology, and it was OK. Plus, I did one production my freshman year.

"I went through college and two years of graduate school with my performance stuff on the back burner. I did some extra work through the one casting agency that's in Pittsburgh, for the TV show *Unsolved Mysteries*, and in the movie *Rob Roy*, but that was it—no dreams of earning my union card or anything like that. I'd gotten interested in pursuing my masters in social work—you're serving human beings in the way of client-centered therapy, but you could change rounds, work in schools, work in prisons. I was interested in that because it would allow that me to play different roles.

"My second year of graduate school, I did my internship at the Children's Hospital of Pittsburgh. I was the trauma social worker—it was quite challenging and fast-paced. Unfortunately, children lost their lives, or were maimed, or had their lives changed forever by traumatic events. As a social worker in an emergency room, you're presented with a huge, horrible situation, and there are all of these poor people connected to it, and you have to manage them and help them while serving your staff. You have to keep it together for everyone—it's very sink or swim. You're just trying to give those families everything you have in the moment. Once I did that for a year, and knew I had the stuff for it, I finished my MSW, sent my resume out, and got a letter back right away from Sinai Hospital in Baltimore. By May 1997, I'd become the pediatric social worker there. It was an extremely awesome, challenging job. By the spring of 1998, however, I was like, oh, my goodness, I need an outlet! I haven't acted in years!

One Sunday, I looked in the arts and entertainment section of the paper, and saw auditions for an Actors' Company Theatre/Chesapeake Center for the Arts production of *Steel Magnolias*. I went to the audition, and got cast. Pretty much, my life just changed! I was working, going to my little play practices during evenings on the weekend, meeting people, making new friends. Of course, the people I was meeting were connected to other theater people, which led to two fun dinner theater things I ended up doing. And it turned out that the director of *Steel Magnolias* happened to be a casting associate for Pat Moran Casting, the major casting agency in Baltimore; they cast for John Waters and Barry Levinson. Everybody around me knew who he was and who he worked for, but, I was like, 'Who's Pat Moran?' I had no idea.

"But through him, I got an opportunity to do extra work on Barry Levinson's TV show *Homicide: Life on the Street*. The whole process of filming that show was so fascinating to me—I just loved it! I told them, 'Any time you want me for anything else, call me! I'll work it out with my job.' But it was always difficult for me to tell the professionals I worked with at the hospital what I was really starting to pursue. There's less stigma involved with saying, 'I'm working on a community theater project,' than, 'I'm taking a day off to work on this movie.' I felt, the more people who know, the more people will think less of me as a professional.

"But I kept pursuing my dream on the side, and by the fall of 1998, got a SAG voucher to work on Barry Levinson's film *Liberty Heights*, with Adrien Brody. I got work for five days, and I thought, I'm doin' this! Adrien just hung out with us, as cool as he could be, and said, 'I'm so excited! I'm in a movie!' And the rest of us were like, 'So are we! But you're a little more important than us!' He's such an amazing actor—I was like, 'Go, boy, go!'

"So from there, I got my SAG card in 1999. I was able to do more stage, to do work with many different directors and companies. I also did *Cecil B. Demented* and then *A Dirty Shame* with John Waters. Oh, my God! John includes so many of his friends and people he's worked with before, so his sets are so comfortable. In

A Dirty Shame, my friend Angela and I played sexoholic twins oppo-site Johnny Knoxville, very fun! I was also Tracey Ullman's stand-in, so I met a lot of people, and it was amazing.

"I started leading the Fells Point Ghost Walk Tour in 2002, too. The girls who run it, Missy and Amy, are these young, awesome entrepreneurs. It's not like taking a crowd through a controlled museum environment—you're walking through public streets, where people are colorful. I use every skill I've got—I'm a social worker and I'm an actor when I'm a tour guide! We do the tour from March to November—I haven't done any stage since 2002, because in a way, the tour is fulfilling my performance artist side—it's like a one-woman show!

"In February 2004, I left Sinai, and now I'm working at a cri-sis therapy agency. We provide crisis intervention for children up to the age of eighteen. It's unlike anything I could have anticipated—it's honestly very dangerous sometimes. We go out into the Baltimore community, do therapy in the homes of children and teenagers, and we work in very drug-ravaged and crime-ridden neighborhoods. We try to support people through crisis situations, then link them to other services, so that they leave us having more support than they did coming in. Where the children I worked with at Sinai had a medical condition that was impacting their psychoso-cial presentation, the children I'm seeing in the community have a psychiatric diagnosis that's usually challenging them. I only follow the children for two weeks, coming in at their darkest hour, support them during that time, then refer them to long-term therapy.

"Basically, here's the way I work: A behavior specialist col-league and myself will go to the homes, meet with clients, and then see any ongoing clients we have from the day before. There could be up to six hours of face-to-face therapy sessions with clients and their families.

"This work is very worthwhile, and more of a commitment. I can't help feel when I'm mediating that this, in a way is like theater. It's managing, juggling, and understanding where a char-acter is coming from, and still being clear with what my role is. I relate authentically to these people—children and teachers will read you like large print if you're not genuine.

"Doing therapy gets heavy. Some days, you need a mental health day, and you have to be clear about what you have to give on certain days. Some of my friends say, 'You should just focus on being an actress instead!' But I'm like, 'That's not any easier. It's the same emotional commitment.'

"Now I've figured out that I just want to be a working actor and keep my foot in the door, and that's it. If I can continue to find joy and challenges in my work, serving families and children, and exercise my acting muscles, that's my success."

four
doing a world of good

We all say we'd like to make the world a better place, but how many people actually get down to business and do it? Actors are one segment of the population that is known for rolling up their sleeves and getting the job done. There are a number of reasons why this could be. Maybe one actress's sensitivity to the plights of others has to do with feeling like an outcast, growing up with weird creative interests while every other girl in her high school wanted to be a cheerleader. Maybe another's had too many friends die of AIDS, so she delivers meals for Project Angel Food. Whatever the specifics entail, the common denominator for these performers is an earnest desire to at least TRY to do some good.

The performers in this chapter have seen the entire scope of their careers take dramatic detours in the name of social outreach.

From the film star who advocates for victims because he remembers his own abuse, to the actor/director devoting himself to the young, to the performer-turned-fierce animal rights activist, to the artist who brings creative expression to the incarcerated, these people have one very rare trait in common: good old-fashioned selflessness.

THE SPIRITED SURVIVOR

Victor Rivers has been a super-achiever from the word go. Born in Cuba, he came to the United States at the age of two. He wowed the sports world by becoming the first Cuban-American to be out for two seasons with the Miami Dolphins, then set his mind to becoming an actor. Which he swiftly did: Melanie Griffith recommended him for a part in the film *Fear City*. He's since racked up roles in *8 Million Ways to Die, Havana, Amistad, The Hulk, What's Cooking?, Twin Peaks: Fire Walk With Me*, and scores of additional movie, TV, and stage appearances.

What's not so obvious about Rivers's success story is the fact that he's a survivor of mind-boggling child abuse. The victim of and witness to violence inflicted upon his family by his father, Rivers took legal action to remove himself from his abuser as a teenager. Rivers has gone to extraordinary effort to help others suffering in similar situations ever since. He's the author of the best-selling memoir *A Private Family Matter*, which he wrote to offer hope to abuse victims everywhere, and in 1999 he became spokesperson for the National Network to End Domestic Violence.

Rivers is justifiably proud that he can dedicate much of his professional life not simply to entertain, but to literally save the lives of other people. Here, he talks about being both an actor and advocate:

"My own self-discovery about wanting to act, to kind of dig inside, started as a kid. I spent a lot of time alone, punished, in my room. To keep my sanity and entertain myself, I would act out all of these adventure stories, and practice dying in hundreds of different ways, which is very interesting, because of course, I've played villains in many films, and I'm always killed off in various ways. It was like early training!

"I went to Florida State University on a football scholarship. They steered me away from drama because of the time commitment. My degree is in criminology; I was probably moments away from becoming an FBI agent or cop, but then I became a free agent draft pick by the Miami Dolphins, and spent a couple seasons with them.

"I had lived with seven families who basically saved my life, starting from fifteen till I graduated from high school. Steven Bauer's was the last family I lived with; they unofficially adopted me. I believe in paying it forward. There's no way I could pay back Steven's family financially for saving my life, helping me reclaim my life, become who I was supposed to be.

"Steven became an actor, and appeared in *Scarface*, among many other films. He was out in Los Angeles, and after I got cut by the Dolphins, he told me, 'If you really want to be an actor, if it's something you really want to pursue, get in a play.' So I did *Marat Sade*, a real crazy play, and somebody saw me, gave me my first real job and my SAG card. I struggled like any other actor. Andy Garcia and I, who are friends, worked at a moving company. There are very few overnight successes in this business; you've got to stick to it, and it's got to be a passion. Over time, I kept getting roles, and started moving up the ladder.

"When I did *The Mask of Zorro*, I was going to work with Sir Anthony Hopkins. We were at the table reading in Mexico City, and there he was, wearing little glasses. When it came time for him to speak, when he opened his mouth, we could barely hear him—he was mumbling. I was going, "He's gonna be Zorro? Oh, my God.' Two days later, we were doing hair and makeup and wardrobe tests, and I was standing outside with a couple other actors and some Mexican day laborers. Suddenly, I see this trailer door slam open. I look up the stairs, and I see these black boots, and these silver-studded pants, and the cape, and there's Anthony Hopkins with a sword in his hand! The Mexican day laborers go, 'ZORRO!' And he goes, 'YES!' He'd put on the clothes, grabbed his toys, and he was the guy. That's what I've learned to do as an actor—I put on the clothes, and I'm the guy. That's what's exhilarating—being able to be somebody else, having the power to do anything.

"I did a movie called *Fled*, with Laurence Fishburne; the first time I met Salma Hayek was on that set, and she was afraid of me. I played a real nasty guy, and was about to do something not too nice, and I didn't want to break character. I do what the moment calls for.

"I would say if there was one experience that really affected me as an actor, it was *Blood In, Blood Out*. It was directed by Taylor

Hackford; this film has an underground cult following. There were seven actors, and we shot inside San Quentin, the maximum security prison, on death row. I spent almost seven weeks in there, and we were not protected or guarded; we had to sign no-hostage policies. We really got to see what prison was like, and I learned two things. One, there's no rehabilitation in prison to speak of. We need to get to these young men and women before they get there. And two, every guy that I talked to had some form of family violence in his past. The current statistic is that 94 percent of those incarcerated have experienced domestic violence, so you can see that it's a learned behavior. From an actor's standpoint, being thrust into this environment was the greatest barometer; I'd never experienced such total immersion into a character. No one knew my real name, only Magic Mike, my character's name. I really got lost in that guy, and it took me a couple of months to shake him. It changed my life, my ideology. I looked around that prison and thought, there but for the grace of God, because that was the direction I was heading.

"A few years ago, I saw a full-page ad in the *New Yorker* about a group called the National Network to End Domestic Violence. I read this story [in the ad] about a girl who'd had her life turned around with the help of this program. I called this friend who's a publicist and said, 'Call these people and ask if they have a spokesperson.' Most of the pioneers of this movement are women; when my friend asked if they had a spokeswoman and they didn't, he said, 'Well, I have one for you,' and was asked, 'Who is she?' He said, 'It's a he.' That took great vision and courage to place a man in the spokesperson's position, as the misconception is that it's a women's issue.

"The second or third speaking engagement I had [on behalf of the group] was in Houston, a big, big fundraiser, a black-tie affair. I gave the keynote, and I was very emotional. It's always raw and very moving on my end. After I was finished speaking, a number of people came up with nice comments. A gentleman walked up to me. I hadn't seen him all night, and I've never seen him again. He was a very handsome, distinguished older gentleman with white hair, a beautiful white beard, in a tuxedo. He stood eye to eye with me, stuck out his hand, and pulled me in real close, and he said, very quietly, 'I have scars all over my body from what my father did to me. I began to heal tonight for the first time.' It was in that moment, I said to myself, 'the power of story can move people.' I realized this was part of my mission—to tell the truth, to help people realize this is everyone's issue, but also to reach out to men who've dealt with this issue.

"There are so many good men who will stand by while domestic violence goes on. As a former athlete, I use the analogy that if there are fifty guys on a team, you've got the Arrest of the Week of one of them, usually for domestic violence or sexual assault. This guy gets a slap on the wrist, and he returns to a hero's welcome. The rest of the team are usually good husbands, good boyfriends, give their free time to charitable causes, but they're not saying anything [to condemn the violence]. So all fifty guys get lumped in. That's why I hope to reach out to men, to say we cannot allow this behavior, because it's the catalyst for all the violence that we fear.

"They say the biggest fears people have in life are death and public speaking. As I'm an actor, I don't really have a fear of getting up there and make a presentation, but I also allow everything to be moment to moment when I'm speaking. I usually have prepared remarks, because it's so emotional for me many times, I have to have those remarks in case I get lost. I try to let things affect me each time differently, yet because I can control my emotions to a certain degree, I don't get up there and just totally fall apart. Then you'd become unintelligible, and no one can relate to that. I must be someone who allows that emotion, but still gets my message across.

"As an actor, we can always hide behind words and character. But when I give a keynote speech, I'm opening up myself and letting you see inside of me—the wounded boy, the angry young man. My story represents that you can truly break the cycle of violence, and that you can really make a difference. Every time I think I'm done making this presentations, then I say, 'We're not even close. We've made great strides since I was a kid, but we have so much more to march on for.'

"Through my advocacy work, it's absolutely helped me as an actor. It's taken away from the time I've been able to act, because if I'm speaking, I'm not available for an audition. Each time I speak, it enriches me as a person, and opens me up as a husband, a father, a friend.

"I've been in a lot of films and had a lot of leading roles. They say that celluloid lives forever, and I've very, very proud of my work. But if I help to create a more peaceful and loving world to live in, then I feel my time here was well-served."

TEACH YOUR CHILDREN WELL

Michael McGarty's childhood memories of his first moments in the theater have inspired the whole course of his professional life. As artistic director of the Harvard, Massachusetts, Community Theatre, a 700-seat facility, McGarty has innovated the local educational theater scene. The Harvard Community Theatre encompasses three divisions—adult, high school, and middle school. This allows McGarty to focus very strongly on the specific training needs of the young people in each age group that he directs; this unusual educational thrust is renowned throughout the New England arts community.

A third-generation theater professional, McGarty vividly recalls his childhood introduction to the stage. "When I was ten, my father took me to one of the last performances of *The Sound of Music* at Broadway's Imperial Theatre," he says. "He took me backstage to see the scenery, props, and F/X, then sat me in the fifth row to watch the show. I was hooked after that."

McGarty graduated from Middlebury College with a masters in French theater. By then, his journeyman experiences led him to act in both New England and in Europe, where, he comments, "I realized early on that I enjoyed directing more than acting." He then set out to gain experience crewing such Broadway productions as *Pippin*. McGarty found himself constantly inspired: "I must have watched Ben Vereen more than fifty times as I worked offstage, and each night, I learned something new from his style and approach. I learned more from watching directors direct and actors act than I could by acting myself." However, he found he still wasn't happy. "I didn't enjoy doing the same work in New York, night after night. The process of mounting a show is what I loved, and educational theater provided just the right balance of quality and variety."

He decided to enter the field. "I took a job at the Broomfield School in 1976, developing a theater program for students," McGarty explains. "It included participating in the Massachusetts High School Drama Festival, which allowed them not only to tour with a production, but also to experience scores of different shows by the by the time they graduated. We performed in a 150-seat theater, and managed large shows ranging from *Barnum* and *The Music Man* to Marsha Norman's *Getting Out*."

Today, through his work at the community theater, it's all about giving students opportunities. "There are classes students can take to prepare for major roles, but those are not a prerequisite," says McGarty. "Anyone can audition, and I have a tendency to double-cast shows so that more students get a chance to perform. I then carefully balance casts with seasoned performers and newcomers so that the quality of the performance doesn't suffer, and the new actors develop their performance skills." He teaches his students the fundamentals of quality theater without relying on big budgets and technical bells and whistles: "In the long run, your work should be about how you touch the audience's hearts and souls, and not how you dazzle their eyes."

McGarty's work on socially relevant topics is quite meaningful to him. "My successes are not really the awards that different shows or actors of mine have won, but rather some of the challenges that I've taken on," he remarks. "I developed a piece with my students about children of divorce that helped them, and their parents, see a side of this tragedy that parents don't usually understand. That's the type of success I value most."

All in all, McGarty couldn't be happier with his career track; it's had good effect on his family life as well. "Watching my daughter grow up loving theater, and then becoming an accomplished actress and director is my greatest accomplishment. Second to that would be all the students who have passed through the program and then gone on to successful careers in the arts. I try to see as much of their work as possible, and I'm always astonished at their growth, and pleased by how much they love what they're doing."

TO THE RESCUE

Annie Hughes became a sensation as soon as she stepped onto the New York City cabaret scene. Hughes started her illustrious singing and performance career by winning two full scholarships to the Eastman School of Music and the Manhattan School of Music, plus a coveted invitation to the Curtis Institute in Philadelphia. She then spent the next thirty-plus years cementing her reputation as one of Manhattan's great musical acts. "In the course of my career, I have been fortunate to perform in every theatrical medium from opera to Off Broadway, regional theater to television and film, Carnegie Hall to cabaret. I have directed, produced, written, and arranged—I've been able to express every aspect of my artistic passion," she says proudly.

Hughes thanks her mom for finding her wonderful singing teachers when she was a young child, and she credits this as a huge success factor: "All thanks to a mother who was savvy, and two parents who supported me in every way." Hughes was obviously influenced in turn to give support; she is devoted to saving abused and abandoned animals. Theatrical opportunities are still there for the taking: a supporting film role, a sold-out concert, great publicity, the possibility of producing a music series. But Hughes today has an additional calling.

Now a highly-respected canine behaviorist and animal activist in Wisconsin, Hughes discusses her newfound second career and the satisfaction it has brought to her life:

"We always had a dog in the house when I was growing up, so I naturally wanted one when I got my first apartment in New York City. My neighbors had a new puppy, the likes of which I'd never seen—a lhasa apso. (I've been in love with the breed ever since.) A girl I worked with coincidentally had a pair that had a litter.

"Maggie was with me for sixteen years. When it came time for me to make the hard decision to let her go, I stayed with her in the vet's office while he put her down. The experience was devastating, and I couldn't bring myself to have another dog for seven years. Every dear little pup that passed me would tug at my heart, and then their whole life would flash before my eyes . . . I was back in that vet's office.

"There finally came a day when my desire to have life back in my care outweighed painful memory, and I started to search the online shelters. Hearts United for Animals (*www.hua.org*) was the first and most compelling. In spite of the fact that I was in New York City and they were in Nebraska, I kept going back to 'visit the dogs.' Eventually, it was just one dog—Duffy, a male lhasa apso. I finally decided he was the one and sent in my application.

"They politely said no.

"I was stunned, and a little insulted that they would refuse me, so I sent them a missive on every dog I had had in my life; I told them about Maggie, and how well I knew the breed. Their response was that they were concerned about sending a dog to the big, bad city, and that apartment living wasn't optimum, but that they would give me the benefit of the doubt since I seemed so great. They sent someone to look at my apartment! The day after this visit, Duffy was winging his way to Newark [airport].

"I became great friends with the mother-daughter team who run the shelter and lobby passionately for the abolishment of puppy mills. I was their liaison in the tri-state area, doing home visits for prospective adopters, and fostering abandoned animals until they could be re-homed. I also adopted a mill dog from them two years after I got Duffy—Chloe was with us for fourteen years.

"In the summer of 2003, I worked for my certification as a canine behaviorist and interned at a shelter in Queens. [That's where] I found Mollie, another lhasa, who I adopted that November.

"Over thirty years in New York, I had ups and downs. However, the feelings I had post-9/11 were more overwhelming than I could have ever imagined. I couldn't find inspiration or true joy anywhere in my daily life.

"In the summer of 2003, I saw a photo on the Web of a house overlooking the ocean in Nova Scotia, and that planted the seed: 'Someday, there's where I want to be.' The seed took immediate root and I decided that 'someday' was NOW. Six months later, I moved from the city to a house by a lake in Wisconsin.

"Since arriving in Wisconsin, I have done obedience training, working with the local rescue group. I have a new addition to the family—Charlie, a 70-pound boxer/shepherd mix. Charlie was severely abused and exhibited deep behavioral problems making him impossible to adopt, and first in line for euthanasia. After an initially difficult rehabilitation, he has made remarkable progress. I was recently elected to the board of the Waupaca County Humane Society, and we are in the process of building a new shelter.

"I finally feel successful as a human being, and that is the key."

FROM THE INSIDE OUT

Buzz Alexander has built a body of work that honors self-expression. As a teacher, performer, filmmaker, playwright, and author of the book *Films on the Left*, about documentary film production in the 1930s, Alexander's projects deal with important issues like the freedom to pursue creative and political vision.

Alexander founded the Prison Creative Arts Project (PCAP) and runs the program in conjunction with the University of Michigan. PCAP gives the incarcerated a chance to find their voices through a wide range of artistic pursuits, ranging from theater to art to poetry and more.

"PCAP started by chance. I was teaching a course on guerilla theater in 1990, and a student who was working with two lifers at the women's prison at the Florence Crane Women's Facility in Coldwater (who were enrolled from prison at the University of Michigan) told me they wanted to take the course. Four of us made a three-hour trip there once a week to talk theater and do improv with these women. At the end, they turned to each other and said we should open this up to the whole prison. We were able to do that; the Sisters Within Theater Troupe has continued since then, and we're working on our twenty-first play now. PCAP is close to its 200th original prison play."

Alexander's theater career has had strong organic roots from the beginning. His experience includes extensive guerilla theater and video projects in Peru, where he has "been influenced by political activists, by theater activists, by liberation theology priests, and by my peasant compadres, godchildren, and urban friends." From his earliest efforts, "the most important thing was that the work I did was based on a belief that people in communities can create their own art about their own issues, and that my presence and resources can contribute to that," he explains. Alexander's dedication to collaboration is further demonstrated by his additional work with the Western Wayne Players, an incarcerated men's theater troupe, in which he co-creates and plays many roles, and through his readings with the Poet's Corner at the Southern Michigan Correctional Facility.

"We're influenced by Paulo Freire, Augusto Boal, Herbert Kohl, and Myles Horton, among others," Alexander says. "We base our work in respect for EVERYONE present, in belief in those we work with (to pull up their creativity, to work together, to get to a performance based on improvisation) and in a process of discovery. We don't work from texts; we build the plays from our own experiences and ideas, create our own characters and plots—we value the lives and inventiveness of those we work with."

PCAP's theater work is highly detailed. "Our process is, in starting a workshop, to come in and at first do all kinds of games and exercises to get everyone comfortable, then move toward some initial acting," Alexander explains. "We include realistic conflict scenes that aren't resolved—the purpose being, theater is based in conflict, and our plays aren't derived from TV or movies we've seen, but from our own lives. Then we ask the actors to come up with ideas for plays, and we put the ideas up in concrete scenes they have in mind. We see if some of the same ideas can go in the same play, and then we begin building that play by adding scenes and characters, by doing character interviews, by asking hard questions about what it is we're trying to convey—what we want the audience to know, and to take away."

The response to the program participants' work has been highly lauded throughout the national arts scene, and by its audience, which is derived both from the prison population, and outside visitors. "A successful workshop means new skills in collaboration, in commitment to others, growth, belief in ourselves, new perceptions and ideas, and knowledge on how one wants to act in this short lifetime," Alexander asserts. "I'm talking about the prisoner participants AND the rest of us. We all need to grow, and we've all got things missing that we can find through a real, vulnerable commitment to this process, and to each other."

Alexander has done a tremendous service to both his creative artists, and those that will benefit from their insight. In the end, he feels, "Our work is both bearing witness and giving people inside a chance to break stereotypes of prisoners by getting their powerful, beautiful, varied work and voices before the public."

five
helping others seek other careers

Sharing hard-earned knowledge—it's an admirable thing to do, no matter what walk of life you happen to come from. So many of the actors I've spoken to who navigated a successful career change express a strong desire to pass on what they've learned to others seeking to better their lives professionally. These folks see such effort as an extremely valuable way of giving back, and they're absolutely right—been-there, done-that guidance is worth its weight in gold.

Some actors end up dedicating their professional lives to helping others realize their true potential. This kind of work requires a great deal of perception, empathy, and logic—qualities the people you'll meet in this chapter have in spades. In their quest to assist others to make a crucial career or life leap, these compassionate, sensible souls speak about the great sense of self-satisfaction that comes with helping others get what they truly need and want. To that I say, relish the feeling—you deserve it, because you're making a huge contribution to the world.

THE TRAILBLAZER

Carol Mannes has always displayed a gutsy, go-for-it spirit. After a highly successful performance career, she enthusiastically tackled new education goals and faced major personal challenges head-on—with total grace and optimism. Mannes is now a social worker at the Actors' Fund in Manhattan, working through the Phyllis Newman Women's Health Initiative to help actresses deal with the professional and personal challenges that mid-life can present. She speaks about her own life changes, and how she applies her wisdom to aid her clients.

"I had my first professional job when I was sixteen, working as a dancer with a line of girls like the Rockettes—we were called the Gay Foster Roxyettes. We traveled all over the country and Canada, working grandstand shows and state fairs. It was really fun. I was definitely bitten. When I got out of high school, I continued working as a dancer, doing club work, and I started to sing, working with a girl trio. I did that for about four years.

"I just really didn't understand the business of the business, so I decided to leave it. I went back home, married a high school sweetheart, and had three daughters. I missed being creative very much, so I co-founded a children's theater, and ran it for ten years while my children were growing up. When my youngest daughter went into school all day, I went back to the industry, started studying acting. I had a successful acting career for about fifteen years. I also had divorced, and remarried a man who was a director and had a commercial production company. I was his executive producer. I also taught at Circle in the Square off and on for over ten years. I did a lot of commercials, two national tours of *Broadway Bound* and *Lost in Yonkers*, and I also did *Broadway Bound* on Broadway at the end of its run. I did regional theater, film, TV—I was one of the arraignment judges on *Law & Order*.

"Then, in 1995, my passion went out. I'd been on the road a lot—you have to go where the work is—and I just got tired of all the traveling. It just wasn't as much fun as it used to be. I missed being with my family; I missed being with my husband. All of a sudden, I felt like I had recovered from this disease! If you're not enjoying the work when you get it, you shouldn't be in the business.

"I started thinking about what else I could do. I had no idea, so I decided to go back to school—I had never finished my undergrad degree. I was living on Long Island at the time, and Adelphi has a very good program for adults, so I went there to finish my degree. I was able to get like thirty credits for my life experience, so I really only had three semesters to finish. One of the professors asked me, 'What are you going to do when you get out? You won't get anywhere with this degree.' I said, 'I don't know.' He said, 'You should get your MSW.' He advised me to go to Columbia. I applied at Columbia, Fordham, and NYU, and got into all three. In the interim, however, my husband was diagnosed with lung cancer, and passed away four months after that. That was a tremendous challenge for me. He was the love of my life, and he was just great.

"I was glad, in retrospect, that I had already been accepted at Columbia; it gave me something that I had to do. It was tremendously healing for me. In social work school, the first year of field placement, they place you, and the second year, they give you a choice of places. When I saw that the Actors' Fund was one of the choices, I thought, this is perfect! I'd been a supporter of the Actors' Fund, but I didn't know they had social work staff. I was able to get here for my second year internship, and then was able to get a position here.

"Sometimes, women will say to me, 'I'd like to go back to school, but I'm too old.' And I can say to them, 'Excuse me, I went back to school when I was sixty. I'm no different from you—if I can do it, you can do it.' I was not very computer-literate when I started at Columbia. A lot of things were done online, and I remember coming home from orientation and saying to one of my daughters, 'I'm not going to be able to do this.' She said to me, 'Mom, you can and you will!' That was great. They had computer labs at Columbia! I also thought, 'I'm going to be so much older than everybody!' But it turned out that the professors liked older students—they can relate better to us. And the students never made me feel I was old. I felt a great camaraderie with them because we were all in the same boat. Once I got over my own perception, I never encountered any kind of bias.

"My focus here is the Phyllis Newman Women's Health Initiative, which assists women who are dealing with serious medical or mental health issues. I find that tremendously rewarding. I help women find therapists; I help women deal with what happens when you get a serious illness. For almost the whole time since I've been here, I've developed and co-run a women's peer support group. It helps women in mid-life deal with all the challenges of aging in this industry. The industry is very cruel to women after forty, and I discovered after seeing clients here day after day that a lot of women hit their mid-forties, they've been successful and given up a lot to be successful, but then the industry says, 'We don't care anymore.' These women feel isolated, and very much like it's their fault, so I co-facilitate this with another social worker here, we do it twice a year, and it's been tremendously helpful for these women to realize they're not alone, to bond with other women. That gives me a lot of satisfaction.

"I'm really very lucky, because this agency allows you to be very autonomous. I'm an early bird, so I like to get in early, get myself organized before a lot of other people are here. Our work hours are 9:30 AM to 5:00 PM, but you don't punch a clock, nobody hangs over you. I make my own appointments—I usually see about two clients a day. All the social workers have group meetings about once a week. One of the things I like about the work is that every day is different, every client is different, and every client's story is different.

"When I first started to go back to school, I had this terrible void. I thought, 'If I'm not a performer, what am I? Who am I?' Your identity is so wrapped up in that. I just decided, though, let's see what happens. I was nervous about change. But I do have a spiritual component in my life that's about letting go. Once everything happened to my husband, I felt that the universe took away something so dear, but said, I'm going to give you something else. I'm very grateful for that, every day. I have wonderful support from my children and sons-in-law, great friends. Every day before I go to sleep, I just think, I'm so grateful for all of these blessings.

"It's a great feeling of pride to know I'm doing good work and helping people, and that other people feel I'm doing a good job. I hope to stay physically and mentally healthy for a long time, so I can keep doing it!"

THE ENLIGHTENED ONE

Compassion, sensitivity, and a highly nuanced world view—these qualities drive the arts work of Daena Giardella. She has lived through some of the most intense experiences life has to offer—from surviving Scud missile attacks in Tel Aviv during the Gulf War, to aiding those affected by the horrors of 9/11—by using her artistic impulse therapeutically, and always with an eye toward giving back to others. Giardella's toured the United States and internationally with her one-woman shows *Yes to Everything*, *Moment to Moment*, *Bare Essentials*, *Play!* and *Now What* (a piece developed with her life partner and collaborator, Wren Ross, with whom she has authored an upcoming book as well).

Also a director, radio host, and motivational speaker, Giardella co-founded TheraVision, a video/theater process for training therapists at the Kantor Family Institute. She also coaches in the areas of creativity, acting, presentation, and media—her clients include Citibank and Kodak, and she's worked at esteemed events including the United Nations Conference on Women.

Here, Giardella discusses how she uses her many diverse gifts to most positively affect the human development of others.

"My creativity coaching arose from both my teaching and performance work. I understood early in my work that before students could learn the skills of acting, they needed to become comfortable in the exploration of their own psychology. It was useless to add layers of acting techniques onto an unexamined self. I found that most of my teaching—whether it was in college theater departments, private classes, or in individual sessions—began with the freeing of each person's body, voice, and emotional make-up. For many years, I taught at Emerson College and Boston Conservatory. The class might have been called scene study or intermediate acting, but the first order of business was helping students discover and OWN their confidence, passion, impulses, and power of imagination. My private coaching (whether I'm working as a creativity coach, presentation coach, or media coach) developed as an outgrowth of my psychological approach to teaching as well as my methods for creating characters in my original performances.

"I look at each coaching session as an improvisation. Each client and I toss impulses, questions, and themes back and forth as we search for new insights and openings. I see my job as a guide who shines a flashlight into the sometimes dark and convoluted tunnels we might encounter along the way. I'm also an improvisational partner who challenges each person to find the important threads of their creative goals as they untangle the inner obstacles that thwart outer success and accomplishment. My intention is to help people feel confident, free, and passionate about expressing themselves creatively. I try to make each coaching session a safe and stimulating laboratory that enables people to give shape to their dreams, ideas, and vision.

"When people call me about my improvisational acting workshops or creative coaching sessions, they often say they're searching for a lost spark of creativity that once filled their lives. They might say that they feel stuck or blocked. Others tell me that they need to recover their humor, spontaneity, or playfulness. They want to loosen up and feel comfortable thinking and speaking on their feet. Some people are bursting with creative ideas, but can't seem to find a structure or form to pour them into. They need help building reliable day-to-day structures that will support a regular creative practice.

"The most common themes I encounter as a creativity coach and teacher are the needs to overcome fear and self-doubt. Many people don't feel they have a RIGHT to create. Creativity is everyone's birthright. I feel that helping each individual feel stronger and more self-assured about exercising his/her creative process is a form of social outreach. Creativity is an act of revolution; it's a path of self-development that catalyzes new possibilities within individuals and communities.

"I'm profoundly moved and inspired each time I witness someone daring to make their dreams a reality as they dedicate themselves to overcoming their inner demons and becoming the fullest human being they can be. This is the reward, the fruit of my labor—the deep satisfaction of being in the presence of an undaunted search for truth. Each time I share such a journey with someone, I feel I've become a little more human, a little more awake to the resilience of the human spirit, and interestingly, I become a little more conscious of my own story.

"I think the reward that comes from coaching someone lies in the revelation of each person's story. Stories heal us and reveal us. They help us put ourselves together as individuals, and each time we hear another's story (or our own), we find a clue that enables us to fit the jigsaw puzzle of our lives into the larger puzzle of humankind. I see coaching, therapy, and theater as variations of the same mission: the creation of safe containers that coax the telling of stories that hold the key to where we came from, who we are, and what we might become. My reward as a coach is the same as my reward as a teacher or actor. I receive the gift of participating in the transformational power of story.

"I've learned that an actor who wants to create original theater has to carry many tools for inner and outer resourcefulness in her bag. One key tool stands out—the ability to dare to make something happen instead of passively expecting opportunities to knock on the door regularly. Rather than waiting for someone to cast me in the role of my life, I resolved to write and CAST MYSELF in the shows I wanted to act in. And I also did not shrink back from producing my own work, even though this can be more than a little stressful and challenging at times!

"I'm sure I've been well-served by my passionate determination to create new forms to support my creative vision. I've never tried to fit into a conventional mold. That quality has forced me to develop skillfulness in dealing with skepticism and resistance.

"I place a great deal of value in the ability to negotiate, dialogue, and collaborate with people from all walks of life who might have very differing perspectives. The cultivation of intelligent, flexible, and empathic communication skills is crucial. Above all, whether we're acting on the stage of life or in theater or film, we need to be excellent communicators if we hope to succeed. I'm sure that my communication skills have helped me open many career doors in widely diverse settings.

"I've always had an unwavering dedication to discovering and expressing the truth. Integrity is a nonnegotiable value for me in work and life. These qualities have become tools that help me discern what's important and what matters most to me.

"Next is the ability to live life as an improvisation. My willingness to take risks by embracing the unknown and the unexpected has been an important tool. We need to develop an ability to find the passionate YES—instead of the defeated NO—when faced with surprising situations, curve balls, or obstacles.

"Finally, I've found that having and regularly exercising a hearty sense of humor has been essential. No matter where I am or what I'm doing, I always have a humor track running in the back or forefront of my mind I look for the sideways perspective that tickles my funny bone and lends some fresh air to a stale room. I think of humor as the buoyancy that keeps us from falling too far into the cracks of life's existential abyss. Laughter helps us regain our footing and remember we're not the only clowns in the circus."

THE TEAM PLAYER

Elaina Vrattos has many strengths. As an actress, she appeared in films like Clint Eastwood's *Mystic River*, made her mark in productions like *Nine, Nunsense, Into the Woods, Fiddler on the Roof*, and *Hot L Baltimore*, and received coveted awards from the New England Theatre Conference and the Eastern Massachusetts Association of Community Theatres. As a producer, her business smarts have led to the success of Big Smile Productions, a Newton, Massachusetts-based theater company.

Now focused on directing, Vrattos succeeds at getting the best out of experienced performers. She's also built a peerless reputation for introducing non-professionals to the world of acting through her community theater work. A true veteran (she's staged scores of shows, ranging from *A Chorus Line* to *The Heidi Chronicles*), Vrattos infuses her casts with confidence, builds a great group dynamic, and makes every newcomer feel like an old pro in record time. Here are the tools she uses to get the job done.

Education and Experience

"I got a full scholarship to Boston University as a drawing major, and my brother was there as an acting student at the same time. I knew I wanted to do theater, too, but I was afraid to do it—I think I was repressed, and I was chubby, and just felt like I was never going to be that type of person. But a high school teacher of mine was producing a play in Boston, and I ended up working on it, and that was it for me. After graduating from college with my art degree, one second later, I was onstage acting, and backstage learning directing.

"I did a bunch of community theater to get started. I worked at Newton Country players, cast in the ensemble of shows, doing *Jacques Brel*, then playing one of the witches in *The Wiz*, doing all these crazy little roles. I started to get more and more into doing costumes, sets, whatever—you roll up your sleeves and do everything in community theater. My cousin then started a group called Charity Productions, where all that organization's show profits were donated to charity, and I started getting a lot of experience directing there, plus acting in more shows."

Persistence

"In 2003, the Turtle Lane Playhouse (a well-known community theater in Auburndale, Massachusetts) was looking for a director for *NINE*. I kept sending my resume to them to direct, and had directed *NINE* before. They kept getting good words on me, but at first didn't want to take a risk, but eventually thought I was a good fit, and I got it. I've directed at least one show a year there since; I've done *Damn Yankees* and *Big River*."

Generosity

"Directing is my substitute for being a parent, almost. It's being a teacher and being a mother, being a nurturer, a way to pass on a part of yourself to someone else. When I direct, I want [my company] to come out of the experience having learned something, and having grown in some way. I can share what I've learned."

Technique

"When I approach character work, I go with what I know. I guide [my newcomers] with what I do, and how I find stuff [when building a character]. I talk to them about my show concept, and how all the characters interact. I try to show them that they can take different physical things from people they know in real life, the way they talk or act. Even if it's taking from people they see on television or in movies, they can use what they know, and adapt it.

"Every character your actor plays has a little bit of that actor in it, too; as a director, you can't avoid that. You are who you are—that's your basis, and you lay out the character on top of that. I tell them how I came to pick them to play their roles—that sort of encourages them to go forward.

"As far as the technical parts of acting, it's all about explaining how you visualize stuff, how you get there, then throwing them into the fire. Walking them through scenes on their feet."

Effective Routine

"A typical day: I go over blocking, and reestablish what I'm going to go over with my cast. The set designer shows up unexpectedly, and

65

so I ask him a few questions, and go over what I am going to do in rehearsal with him. Then the cast shows up. We're in the early, early stages of rehearsal at this point, so the way that I work is I very loosely block through the whole show, just telling them how they're going to come onstage, where they're going to go, how it's going to look, their exits, all that. It's a lot of getting-to-know-you, a lot of bonding, a lot of them trying to understand me and who I am through talking through the show. The actors have to have confidence, and an understanding of what I want, before I can get them up there, especially at this level. I mean, if I was working with all professionals, I might not handle it like this at all, but since 90 percent of my cast is not professional, and one of my leads has never done a part like this at all and is mostly a singer, you've got to get rid of their inhibitions and make them feel comfortable."

Attention to Detail

"At Turtle Lane, you've got one show up while you're rehearsing another, so I can't really do a lot on the stage with another set there. So (initially) I'm doing a lot of talking through the script, walking through scenes—(then) I can really delve into characters and minutiae blocking."

Appreciation

"I feel like I've done what a lot of people in the world don't get a chance to do, and that is, really know that I've changed people's lives!"

THE TROUPER

Amy Dolan Fletcher has lived the dream of many—she started her successful performance career as a mere child, and worked consistently for twenty-five years. Now, as the national education and outreach coordinator for Actors Equity, Dolan Fletcher dedicates her time both to the orientation of new union members, and to traveling the country presenting career information and options to students interested in a possible stage career. She speaks with honesty and intelligence about both the challenges and joys a new career track can bring:

"I began performing professionally when I was seven. I did a lot of commercials and theater. I did the Radio City Christmas show for a long time. Then I went to Fordham and sort of relaunched my career again after I graduated college, as an adult. I did many regional theater productions, then the national tour of *Grease*. I made my Broadway debut in Tommy Tune's production of *Grease* when I was twenty-five. I did the Harold Prince production of *Showboat* in the West End. I also got cast in the Broadway revival of *42nd Street*, so I got to do the original cast recording and the Tony Awards.

"Then I decided to look for another kind of job; I was getting married. So I went to the Actors' Work Program, and Career Transition for Dancers. I went through their process, and knew I wanted to do something related to theater—I'd had my own production company, had done a lot of seminars, and provided corporate entertainment. Basically, just through talking with Patch and Kathy at the Actors' Work Program, they would help me frame my application or resume in a way that was best-suited to a particular job, or would put me in touch with the right people. Kathy was amazing; I would send them resumes and cover letters at midnight, saying they had to be in the next day, and at one o'clock in the morning, she'd write notes for me.

"The strange thing about this job is that it's basically the only job in the universe where I'm not allowed to audition, because it's a conflict of interest. It's been a little bit of a difficult transition, knowing I don't even have that option. I've been at this job since August 2004, and it's the longest I've ever gone without being in a theatrical production. I also got married in October 2004, and moved from Manhattan out to Long Island, so it's been a big change. It's not lost on me that I got the only job in the universe where I couldn't audition; part of it has been very freeing, because I just can't, so I've kind of turned off that part of my brain, and I'm looking for other ways to express myself and be creative. I'm going to direct a community theater production, and see where that leads me.

"I think the most difficult part is living at level five instead of level ten. I do a lot of presentations, and when I do one for a group of students, there's only so much you can give. It's almost like you have to shut down a little bit. Because I have to do a lot of stuff with committee members, in the corporate environment, where nothing gets done in any sort of timely fashion; I'm used to a much more rapid pace. The biggest critique I've received here is that I'm over-enthusiastic, which up until now has been a positive. It's a different mindset.

"I spend a lot of my day scheduling, answering e-mails and questions from members, and trying to come up to with new ways to do things. Writing brochures, writing letters to schools to have me come in, canvassing. I also talk to liaisons across the country, to try to get them to work with me when I come to their cities, so that maybe they can set up some schools, or some events I can attend. There's a lot of juggling. I also am usually traveling. For example, next week I leave early Wednesday morning, go to Detroit, and I'll do a presentation at Wayne State, and then the next day I'm flying to the University of Iowa to do a presentation there. In addition to the students, I work with members on member education—I send out postcards for a new members' reception—there's a little bit of event planning, too.

"Getting to go out and share my experience with up-and-coming students is the best. It's nice to see their spark, and remember that I did used to really love [theater]. It's also nice for me to be able to give a certain reality. All I thought I wanted to do was be on Broadway, because that's all I knew as a goal. In truth, if I really look at my skills and interests and the way I operate as a human being, I maybe would have been better off singing with a big band. I don't regret anything I did, of course; I had these other abilities, and I was sort of on this track, but I never really sat down and thought, 'How much money am I going to make? What's my day-to-day life going to be like?'

"I think what the students I talk to want to know is what the 'answer' is. There is no formula. It's just all really in the doing. I was always so busy looking for the next job, I had one foot out the door. I feel like the few moments I had when I was REALLY in the moment were golden.

"I felt like I couldn't stay in show business and get married. I felt those things were mutually exclusive. I don't want to go out and be on the road in my first year of marriage—it seems like that's shooting myself in the foot, because day to day is when I need to build what I'm going to have for the rest of my life. I didn't realize it was just as important to put time into that as going to a tap class or a singing lesson. I can't imagine right now being in a Broadway show and trying to maintain a house and a husband and a dog.

I think about if I want to have children, and where that would put me. I feel that at this time in my life, this is what works best for me.

"Looking for a job, I think the ones that suit you start to kind of sparkle a little bit. You think, oh, that's something I would really be good at. You start to build confidence in the fact that you're ahead of the game when it comes to a lot of jobs. So many actors say to me, 'I don't have any skills besides being an actor. The truth is, you're 80 percent there, because so many people don't show up, aren't dedicated, don't have a work ethic, don't know how to present themselves. Also, realize that nothing is forever. You're not a failure. You're not giving up on your dream—you're taking a different path, possibly back to the same place. It's gonna be tricky, but it's like a new role—it can be just as exciting to navigate your way through looking for a job, having an interview.

"Ultimately down the line, the respect you get for your intelligence, the steady paycheck, all of those things can really make you a better actor, or help you realize that maybe you have another dream. There are days when it really hurts, but there are also days in theater when it really hurts. Everything has its ups and downs.

"I'm not so good with change. I think the tool you have to have is positive self-talk. And to not get lost in a job, either. I think as an actor, you have a tendency to throw yourself in entirely, because that's what you have to do. But you have to learn to slow down and say, everything is OK today. I can take things slowly, one thing at a time. I don't have to be a tremendous multitasker. [A new job] is a break, really.

"You have to find joy within yourself. You're not your career. You're yourself."

six
share what
you know

Actors are often advised to get a teaching certificate to "to fall

back on." It's easy to see why this advice is so often given—

teaching requires great public speaking skills, excellent text com-

prehension and interpretation, and a talent for improv in those

think-on-your-feet-because-this-class-is-totally-out-of-control

moments. Sadly, many actors see teaching as a compromise,

though. They figure it's an "acceptable" alternative only if they

don't make it big, and fail to realize the amazing creativity it can

actually afford.

The actor-teachers in this chapter have plumbed the depths
and corners of imparting education from every angle, and gain great
joy from the doing of it. One is an esteemed Ivy League drama
department head; one a highly respected teacher of younger kids;
one runs a hot industry training school; one is a teaching artist; and
one is actually a writer of informational books gleaned from his

years as a performer living in the Big Apple. All feel pride in the value of passing along the lessons they've learned as actors, and from the diverse lives they've led.

A LIFE LESS ORDINARY

Ellen Kaplan traveled a long, hard road to become a professor and chair of the theater department at Smith College. As a young girl, she had a difficult home life; her mother suffered from mental illness, and Kaplan was an abuse victim as a result of this. Fending for herself in the world, she found drama to be a crucial form of self-expression, and enjoyed tremendous success as an actress. She explains how her talents and sensitivity led her to teach and inspire others:

"Theater was never what I considered a 'career.' Rather, acting and writing were means, I can see in retrospect, of claiming an identity, of building a self and a soul. Certainly, they were healing activities. I was very wild as a teen, involved in fairly self-destructive behaviors. I chafed at college, and left to travel in Europe. When I returned, I majored in theater simply because it gave me pleasure, but still I had no career plan.

"Here's what happened in my twenties. I read voraciously. I wrote every day (educational texts and audio/visual programs for Education Design, a publishing house in New York). I studied with a demanding acting teacher, Bill Wendt, whose work was deeply grounded in Stanislavski. I continued the Lessac voice work I'd done in college, and I took classes in movement with Loyd Williamson, whose work opened my breathing and helped me to live in my skin, fully to the edge. I spent a year in Rhinebeck, as an actor with Larry Sacharow's Open Studio, and explored what it meant to be part of a theater collective. The company received training in drama therapy and other skills, and worked with the elderly and disadvantaged youth, in addition to a full performance schedule. The experience was completely exhilarating.

"After several years of writing (I returned to my freelance work with Education Design, which I continued for many years), studying in New York, getting my union cards, and working in both New York and in regional dinner theaters, I decided I needed to leave New York. The business aspect of acting was not for me—I had no desire to figure out how to 'sell myself.' And the city's pressures combined with my own high-gear personality to create a non-stop work life, which was exhausting me. I wanted immersion, yes, but balance, too.

"I was preparing to move to Seattle when Bill Wendt asked me to join him at Greensboro College in North Carolina, where he was now heading the MFA acting program. In exchange for teaching what turned out to be a full load of voice and acting classes, I would enroll in the MFA program. Going to Greensboro was a purely practical decision. I had no interest in obtaining an advanced degree, nor in teaching. I accepted the invitation simply because it was time to leave New York—if teaching was part of the package, so be it.

"And imagine my surprise—teaching was as exhilarating as acting! Clearly, this new work drew from the same sources—my imagination, intellect, and passions were fully engaged. Teaching was fully creative, and I was growing as an artist and as a person, finding new parts of myself that were wild and nurturing, absorbed in others yet deeply in touch with myself. The rawness of acting, the honesty—things I cherished and sought in myself—I could entice them from others. The young BFA students were fired up with curiosity and energy and powerful imaginations, yearning to develop craft through questioning, exploration, and daring. My questions were their questions, and as I taught, I learned and grew. This was astonishing to me! I was as free—freer—in the classroom than onstage.

"I continued to teach. For many years, the answer to the question I regularly put to myself—why am I teaching—was: I teach because I have so much to learn. I've now been teaching for over twenty-two years, and several years ago, that answer no longer seemed to suffice. Not that it's no longer true, but simply, it was no longer the central reason I taught. I now believe that what I strive for in teaching is the production of joy. That's my mantra now, it's what keeps me going, and it's what I believe.

"Success means having a student, at the end of the first acting class this semester, come up to me, hug me and really mean it, and say, 'I LOVE you!' That was fantastic. It means the class MATTERS somehow.

"I think my soul would shrivel without this work. You can't be alive in a classroom, or on a stage, and be joyless or cruel or self-absorbed. So it keeps you alive. It keeps your imagination dancing—to be WITH others the way you must if you are teaching."

OH, VERY YOUNG

A respected stage actress and director, Sherri Allen has worked at the La Jolla Playhouse, the Old Globe Theater, North Coast Repertory, and PCPA Theaterfest; most recently, she understudied all the female performers, including Amanda Plummer, in Emily Mann's production of *Uncle Vanya*. Currently, she also teaches drama to grades K-12 and English at the middle and high school level in the San Diego school system. Here Sherri talks about her core educational beliefs, and the knack she has for inspiring creativity in her littlest charges.

Q: What motivated your interest in teaching?

A: My mom was a teacher. Apparently, something rubbed off, because when I was a captain/performer specialist at Legoland, training novice actors and directing shows for special events, I was frequently complimented on my instruction. The young performers said, "You're really good at this; you make it easy to understand. You should teach." I was flattered, but my mother warned me that teaching could be a difficult, frustrating, and an unrewarding experience. Alternately, she encouraged me to get a teaching credential as something to fall back on (the old adage). Everyone knows it's difficult to become an actor, but I had been a working actor for twenty years. So becoming a teacher was a lifestyle choice; I didn't do it out of necessity.

I approach teaching from the perspective of a performing actor. Theater can be used as an impetus for social change; it teaches individuals that they can make a difference in their communities by encouraging political activism. Participating in theater is clearly a political act, because theater educates.

Q: Can you describe your philosophy/strategy for teaching kindergarten/lower elementary school grades?

A: Henry Giroux once said, "Without hope, there is only the politics of cynicism." My philosophy of teaching integrates hope, caring, and a sense of the possible, so that I nurture my students in their discovery of themselves and their world. Every child has a right to learn. I set the bar high enough so that my students challenge themselves, and I make accommodations for those who need extra support to reach their goals. My job is to help my students understand themselves in the process of becoming, to help them explore and open up all the possibilities that the world has to offer them. I strive to build an environment of trust and mutual respect so that meaningful work can take place, because risk-taking can only happen in a safe and nurturing atmosphere. I believe that learning can and should be an enjoyable experience. It's my desire to insure that every student has that voice in my classroom.

Conducting courses for young children, I realize they have very short attention spans. The younger the age group, the shorter the attention span, so I change up the activities more frequently. My strategy is to change up the activity about every five minutes for the very young.

It's important that I model the behavior I seek, so I demonstrate and give lots of examples. I tell them explicitly what I am looking for or what they will be graded on. I set very clear expectations. They should clearly understand what I am asking them to do. Young children are completely uninhibited, and it is easier to get them to commit fully to an activity or exercise than older children. Older students have become self-conscious; they don't want to look silly in front of their peers. Young children love to look silly in front of their peers—the sillier, the better!

I always grade my students on their effort, not their ability. There will always be a wide variety of abilities in each class. What is important is the effort and growth of each child, not the innate skills they already possess. I always start critiques with lots of positive feedback, and then include one or two things they can work on or improve on for next time. It is important not to overwhelm them with notes. I model this form of critique so that when I solicit peer feedback, the students know how to be supportive, and how to give constructive criticism.

Q: How do you define overall professional success for yourself?

A: What I think of as success is being able to have a life in the theater, and in the arts in general. Fame is fleeting. I have students who have no idea who Olivier was. On the one hand, it breaks my heart. On the other hand, it puts things into perspective. We live in a culture that is obsessed with fame and money, but what I think of as success is enjoying the life you have, and enjoying the journey. As an actor, this means enjoying the richness of the experience, the luxury of different roles, the honor of being allowed to step on the stage, and the tremendous duty and responsibility that we owe the audience."

DIAMONDS IN THE ROUGH

Since 1976, Rita Litton has used her extensive stage and commercial performance experience to train the next generation. ACTeen, her highly esteemed company, is a true industry leader in actor-training workshops for teenagers and young adults at all levels of ability. ACTeen's grads have found success on Broadway, in major motion pictures, on soaps, and in TV ads.

Litton personally has studied at the American Conservatory Theater and the American Academy of Dramatic Art, and acted at the Boothbay Playhouse, the American Players Theater, and with the Great Lakes Shakespeare Festival in the first American production of *The Life and Adventures of Nicholas Nickleby*. Her curriculum spans the full gamut in polishing her talent: acting, improv, voice, musical theater, directing, film technique, commercial technique, scriptwriting, Shakespearean acting, movement, speech, and audition technique classes are all offered.

Starting ACTeen sprang from a specific experience she had as an actress. "I was doing voiceovers and narration in New York for PBS-TV's *Big Blue Marble*," recalls Litton. "The casting director had just started teaching a small group of children on-camera for the Weist-Barron School, and asked if I wanted to help. I jumped at the chance, because at the time my on-camera commercial auditions were less than stellar. I needed to see what I was doing on camera played back, and understand what the casting directors meant when they told me to 'tone it down.' I was a classically trained actress from a prestigious conservatory program and I couldn't book a commercial?! My successful commercial actor friends were living very well, and I realized commercial bookings were the bread and butter of the acting business.

"It didn't take me long to understand what I was doing wrong, but the bigger realization was that working and doing improvs with students was a blast. I was immediately asked to teach my own class, and very shortly approached to develop a special teen curriculum. After a few years, I realized I was teaching a distinctive, and different approach from the adult school, based more on my theater and acting training. I wanted to formalize that distinction with my own program, curriculum, courses, and identity. The division was referred to as 'ACTeen.' It was initially difficult breaking away from the Weist Barron name and identity, and there are still those who incorrectly use the names interchangeably. However, I have maintained excellent relations with Weist Barron for over twenty-five years, and continue to rent their studios for ACTeen classes."

Litton is very hands-on in terms of supervising every aspect of the school. She starts an average day by checking her e-mail. Today's issues: casting director Penny Du Pont, who is working with the NYU graduate film school, wants to have her students visit ACTeen to find potential acting talent for their film projects. Litton sends back word agreeing to work with her students. Next e-mail: Ellen Parks, another casting director, is seeking four teenagers to appear in a film by esteemed director David O. Russell. Litton responds in the affirmative, then gets busy contacting her students' parents for permission, and discusses coaching options with one ACTeen alum in particular. She reviews the film's sides and breakdown when it is available.

Litton then gets started returning a long list of calls. These include calling a teen actor's personal manager, an author requesting that Litton write a cover blurb for a new book, parents looking for feedback on their teen actor's progress, plus an array of former students seeking info on everything from manager searches to college audition monologues to modeling pageants.

Next, Litton tackles paperwork: she attends to application specifics for the upcoming National Foundation for the Advancement of the Arts' ARTS Awards, finishes payroll and tuition duties, and organizes enrollment details for her school's instructors. She then moves on to a variety of media commitments: making arrangements with *Backstage* for an ad, going over the specifics of an upcoming *Ross Reports* cover article, and working on ACTeen's newest publication, *The ACTeen Commercial Audition Textbook*. Litton also consults with the Web designer for ACTeen's Web site regarding new postings, revisions, and bio updates for her successful alumni.

Litton's next order of business: re-read *Mrs. Warren's Profession*, to review a scene for monologue coaching. She reviews her student lists for ACTeen's Advanced Scene Study workshop, partners up the class, photocopies scenes and handouts, and works on her lesson plan. She does a variety of prep work for her teachers, including printing attendance sheets and checking supplies of textbooks and brochures, and reminds them to make notes during the semester for student evaluations. Litton even personally checks the restrooms for supplies and cleanliness.

As students and their parents arrive, Litton welcomes them, hands out written information, supervises tuition collection, then starts her own long teaching day: from 9:30 AM to 3:30 PM. She touches base with her instructors on a variety of pressing issues after classes, returns phone calls from students who were out sick today, then tidies the acting studio and makes sure all equipment is turned off. Then—and only then—does she head for the train home.

The days are long, but her job satisfaction makes them worth such major effort. "I think the most rewarding aspect of my job is creating an atmosphere where actors feel free to 'play,' " she says. "As an actress, I worked with many professional directors through the years. The ones I enjoyed the most, or wanted to work with again, were those who inspired me to take risks, and who gave me freedom to explore. I ask a great deal from my students, so I am thrilled when they rise to the challenge and do something unexpected or brave. That exhilaration, that sense of adrenaline pumping, when the work takes flight . . . that is any director or teacher's goal.

"Of course, I'd love it if some successful graduate would thank me profusely during their upcoming Oscar acceptance speech. Or better still, write a role for me, a la Lee Strasberg in *The Godfather, Part Two*. However, barring that unlikely occurrence, I'll take the student who leaves my class excitedly about the new 'breakthrough' he just had. Or the one eager to explain all that went on to her parent or boyfriend—who can't wait to come back next class and try it all over again—that's terrifically rewarding.

"The famous stage actress Ellen Terry quoted the three *i*'s necessary for an actor's success: intelligence, imagination, and industry, and of these she thought imagination was the most important," says Litton. "I'd copy her list, but probably have to add: organization, organization, and organization. And perhaps integrity. There are many people struggling to maintain businesses in the arts. Temptation exists to lower standards, inflate egos, or make bizarre promises in the hopes of attracting clients, students, and income. Perhaps I am old-fashioned, but I believe your reputation must be spotless. Conflict of interest should be avoided at all costs, and principles take precedence over gain. We are in the arts because we love the work, and want to inspire others to love it as well. They won't love it if they are cheated, scammed, given shoddy treatment, or disrespected."

COMMITTED TO CREATIVITY

David Shookhoff's reputation precedes him as one of the New York theater world's most respected figures. A graduate of Yale Drama School, Shookhoff spent over twenty years as a freelance stage artist. His directing credits include Arthur Miller's *A View from the Bridge* and Romulus Linney's *Can Can*; his educational experience includes teaching acting and directing at Sarah Lawrence, Columbia, and the University of Pennsylvania.

Shookhoff's intense dedication to the concept of inspiring new artists led him to work at the Lincoln Center Institute during its exciting formative period. In 1989, he helped found the Manhattan Theatre Club's distinguished Education Program, and continues to serve as its director. The program, which targets high school–level students and above primarily, uses teaching artists proactively to introduce students to the craft of theater, gives young people access to challenging live MTC performances, provides classroom teachers with a better ability to implement and use arts education, and encourages students' interest in theater management careers. Here, Shookhoff talks about his own professional career track, and discusses the rewards to paying creativity forward so effectively.

"For the first twenty years [of my career], I was living by my wits as so many of us do in the arts, going from job to job. Even before that, though, as I was leaving Yale, I came across some opportunities to work as an artist in schools, as a professional developer. I came to this from two motives; one, of course, was to flesh out the mosaic of a freelance career, to supplement income, but also, because it increasingly became such an interesting and challenging prerogative, to think about what theater should be and how to bring it to kids.

"After I left Yale, I was teaching at the University of Pennsylvania, and through a contact I'd made, I was working with the education program at the American Shakespeare Theatre. That morphed into something called the Center for Theatre Techniques and Education. The woman who ran it, Mary Hunter Wolf, of sainted memory, sort of saw the handwriting on the wall at AST, and had made her own operation an independent not-for-profit. Then, when I came to New York in the early 1970s, I got involved with what is now the Lincoln Center Institute. Lincoln Center, Inc., had a broad educational mandate as part of its incorporation, and I was part of a group of folks who began to identify and develop the theory and practice that was embodied by the mid-1970s in LCI.

"It was exciting on two levels. The Lincoln Center program worked with kids of all age levels, K-12, and there were relationships with institutes of higher learning, and teachers in terms of professional development. So you're talking about a huge range of clientele, different mindsets, different objectives, and different agendas—for myself, the teaching artist, and the institution we were serving. It was about keeping on your toes! So there was that intrinsic excitement of lighting up those populations, and also the intellectual challenge. I think the field of arts education to this day hasn't grappled with some of the fundamental issues of theater education. I think we're somewhat clear about the 'hows'—how to do it, how to get a class excited and engaged—but the more difficult questions of policy, theory, and advocacy, we're not all that sophisticated about to this day. Why is it important for a child between the ages of five and eighteen to study theater, for example? In this environment of high-stakes testing and days that are so packed full of competing needs and agendas, math, and literacy, what is the place of the arts? To kind of grapple with those kinds of questions has been an interesting theoretical exercise, quite apart from the moments of seeing those light, joyful faces in the classroom.

"So the Lincoln Center program was something I was doing on a freelance basis, as my whole life was! Running around the country, doing *Romeo and Juliet* in Tennessee or whatever. One of the places where I'd begun my freelance career was at Manhattan Theatre Club, in its embryonic years. MTC was coming of age in the early seventies as I was, and a bunch of us from Yale—Lynne Meadow among them—sort of gravitated toward MTC when it was a fledgling showcase operation on the East Side. We were doing these kind of contemporary operas at that time there, while I was also making my way freelance around the country, as MTC was maturing. At a certain point, I came to the realization—as a worker, a parent, a mortgage holder—that it was time to settle down and get a job! MTC, similarly, was coming to the realization that it needed to be serving the community in other ways than simply producing seven plays for a subscription audience per season. Barry Grove, our producer, understood this, and the solution was to start an education program. It was a confluence of a bunch of different needs, desires, backgrounds, and experiences.

"Barry and Lynne asked me to see what I could do, in regard to an education program. What I essentially did do was bring a lot of the thinking and practices I'd been part of developing at LCI to MTC. Both LCI and MTC's philosophical choices are to create programs that put the work of art at the center. That was something I came to feel passionately about, that it is an extraordinarily powerful approach for bringing arts to students—to have informed encounters with works of arts, theater in particular. It was an easy kind of transition for me, both practically and theoretically, to take some of those ideas and bring them here. We got a play grant from the state arts council, I identified a couple of schools with which I'd had prior relationship work, and we began some pilot programs, in-class workshops. These workshops allowed students to come to see plays at our theater, and have a richer, more meaningful, more powerful experience.

"A model that we've grown over the years had to do with X number of workshops in the classroom, hands-on, theater-based, which prepared the kids for the play they were about to see; the expectation that the classroom teacher would carry the work forward between a teaching artist's visits, the teaching artist in the early years being me; and that together, we'd develop and go teach this unit of study that would enrich the students' experience in seeing the play. We were in that sort of pilot phase for about a year and a few months; Barry then went to a foundation connected to MTC's then–chairman of the board, and got a big multi-year gift. That really put the education program on solid financial footing. So we began in spring 1989 with a less than $10,000 grant from the state's arts council, plus matching funds to create a budget of about $20,000, and now we're moving toward a budget of $1.5 million.

"We began to supplement with other program components— professional development; a family matinee program, where we invite seventy-five kids, each with an adult, to one of our main stage productions; Project Interact, where two schools pair up to do preparatory workshops jointly; and Write on the Edge, our playwrighting program, using attending a play as a springboard for students to bring a little embryonic writing of their own to fruition—at the culmination, we do a festival. Another major component is Theatre Link, our Internet-based program. We have an international school in Greece, and we use a specially created Web site to communicate with fifteen different high schools, who collaborate in groups of three, so there are five different projects going on. Working with teaching artists, the students study a play—this year, it's *Brooklyn Boys* by Donald Marguiles, which we produced last year—via video clips on the site, and scripts. They then use that play as a springboard to create their own original plays for part of the semester, then in the final phase, pass their plays to partner schools, who produce them. We also have an afterschool playwrighting program for students who are seriously interested in writing that David Auburn leads, called Write Now.

"When I look for teaching artists now, they need to really have their chops, both as artists and in the classroom. The folks I work with tend to have established careers in both areas. I'm really looking for teaching artists who are experienced as actors, in high-quality professional situations. Beyond that, they need to have the ability to communicate effectively, to talk with teenagers, and work with them. That means a certain kind of self-confidence and expertise, the ability to be flexible, to put up with a certain kind of frustration that comes when dealing with the complication of a massive education bureaucracy. A sense of humor! These are skills that not every good artist possesses—many extraordinary actors don't have the temperament.

"There's always an extraordinary excitement I feel when a group of kids come to see material that would seem remote, alien, and not of their world, and I see them get really jazzed. One play that we did relatively early on, Caryl Churchill's *Mad Forest*, begins with the cast lined up along the footlights, shouting at the audience in Romanian. The whole idea of bringing a group of inner city teenagers into that experience without the extensive preparatory work we'd done would send the kids running for the exits! But the kids were engaged. We also did Alan Aykbourn's *Absurd Person Singular*, a 1970s British comedy about social mobility—not the sort of thing, again, you think teenagers would be groovin' on. But by the end of the play, the kids were cheering, and at the curtain call, made the cast feel like rock stars! And to see a kid walk out of the theater, hug her teacher, and say, 'Thank you for bringing me to this play!'

"The whole idea of seeing a student who's had very little positive reinforcement or success in schoolwork, or in life for that matter, almost visibly swell with pride when his or her work is being performed by professional actors before an admiring audience of peers—it's extraordinary! In this job, you feel like you have done something good on most days, or at least by the end of each week— which is what's gratifying."

THROUGH A CHILD'S EYES

Cherene Snow truly uses her talent humanely. An extremely suc-cessful film, TV, and stage actress (her New York theater credits include *Broken-Down Broadway* and George Street's *Public Ghosts, Private Stories*), Snow dedicates a large portion of her time to her work as a teaching artist for primarily elementary school students. Her commitment to encouraging the talent she sees in children is of immense value, both to herself and to her students' personal development. She speaks about why she came to teach, and her technique.

On Her Background

"I got interested in acting at thirteen, in Chicago. My older sister was going to an audition, and I found out about it and wanted to go, too, so my mother took both of us. We auditioned against each other for the same role. I got it a week later, and my sister said the sweetest thing: 'I'm glad that you got the part, because I don't think I would have been able to do it.' I have a great sister.

"I studied drama, and got a BS in theater from Illinois State University. I did theater in Chicago, including *Playboy of the West Indies*, an adaptation of *Playboy of the Western World*. That was a won-derful experience."

On Her Experiences as an Actress

"In 1989, I auditioned for and got cast in the film *The Long Walk Home*, with Whoopi Goldberg and Sissy Spacek. I did that in Montgomery, Alabama, and after I finished I asked myself whether I wanted to go back to Chicago. I wasn't Equity, because in Chicago, it was so much more productive and efficient—there was so much non-Equity work to be had. I decided to move to Los Angeles instead.

"For the next nine years there, I did film and television, and was nominated for an NAACP Theater Award, and won two or three other awards. Then I moved to New York to do theater. When I was living in LA, I'd also done children's theater, and here there was a show called *Letters to Harriet Tubman*, that was owned by Paul Morse Productions. He is deceased, but his father and sister worked to keep the show alive, and after a few years I acquired the rights to it; I've done it here in New York through Urban Stages. I've also gone to Scotland to act at the Edinburgh Festival— it's such a beautiful, beautiful place. The people were very, very wonderful. I got to meet a lot of British actors, see them work, and did a couple of workshops with the Royal National Theater, plus met some actors from South Africa—oh, my goodness! Their bodies are truly their instruments, and they use them to the fullest. They are just amazing."

On How She Started Teaching

"Back in Chicago, I'd also taught theater games and improvisation through an organization called Urban Gateways. They mainstreamed arts into the public schools; it's so important that kids be able to express themselves. I remember one time, I was teaching second grade, and after class, I was leaving the school. The kids were lined up to go to lunch. I walked down the stairs, and one little girl broke out of the lunch line, ran over to me, and just wrapped her arms around my waist. That's when I knew the impact I had. It was so gratifying and moving—I was being of service. I never forgot that. It's one thing to be onstage and get immediate validation, but it's something else when you touch a child's life.

So I got involved with becoming a teaching artist through the Actors' Work Program. I went in, did the orientation, and signed up. I'd go in, I had a counselor, and they'd advise me on how to find work. I took a free teaching artists' workshop through them—it was three weeks, and then after that you'd get your certificate. Tess Parker, who was there at the time, offered a resume workshop that really helped me in getting my teaching artist resume together. They're wonderful, and I tell people to go there all the time. The program is such an amazing tool."

On the Positive Results She Gets with Students

"I find for myself that I truly, truly love teaching first grade, second grade. They're so impressionable at that formative age, and it's so important to have a positive influence—and I know I am a positive influence. It's so good to get them then—they're so raw. For them to realize that they have an outlet, that they have talent, and that they have a way of expressing themselves."

"How I teach depends on what a particular program asks for. If they're going with my curriculum, I always introduce vocabulary, every time I go in, say over a six-to-eight week program. Depending on what grade I'm teaching, I'll do one set thing per day, such as animal sounds, being an animal and turning that into an improvisation. We do various theater games, such as being a machine: one student will start a movement, that movement will be a mainstay, and then every other student will come in and add on whatever their movement is, with everyone touching in some way to form the machine. There are many more theater games, of course; it all has to do with paying attention, following directions, trust, communication. We add all of those things into class as well. What the end result of the workshop is: having them create their own improvisation. To learn acting techniques, terminology, to learn breathing from their diaphragms, sense memory, emotional recall. We incorporate all of that, and the students realize that everything that happens in life has potential for your acting technique. Everything that's happened in a child's life shapes who they are up to the present moment, and who they will become. I use all of those experiences to help them be better people, better students, better actors."

On Her Personal Strength

"I am truly a survivor. This business can be a challenge financially, emotionally. But I know this is my passion. This is something I would pay people to let me do. It's my calling. I have no problem engaging people to do things. You have to be that as a teacher, you had to be that as a person.

"My best friend Oscar P. Grant is a wonderful screenwriter, playwright, and director, a jack-of-all trades and a master of every single one of them. He would always tell me before an audition, 'Let them see your personality.' And it's true—you go up for a commercial audition, you only have thirty seconds. Are you someone they want the entire day working with? So I have personality galore! Those are the things that work for me."

"First, you have to know who you are as a person. I was in LA for nine years, and I ran across people who would lose their minds over things, saying, 'My agent hasn't called!' or 'I need to lose weight!' You have to be all right with yourself exactly how you are! Your thought process has to be about your talent, and then other people will pick up on it.

"Have someone who keeps talking to you when you think, at some point, that it's not happening the way you want it to happen. Having a friend like Oscar who knows the scope of my talent—I met him when he was my director—is a great support system!

"Have passion. Know that you have talent, and that you can do everything. I know the extent of my talent more than my agents do—that's a statement and a fact."

KNOWLEDGE IS POWER

Craig Wroe is not only a critically acclaimed actor, he also shares his knowledge as an instructor at New York City's School for Film and Television. Yet his desire to educate aspiring actors in Manhattan doesn't end there. Wroe is also the author of three well-received books: *Living $mart—New York City: The Ultimate Insider's Guide*, *An Actor Prepares . . . To Live in New York City: How to Live Like a Star Before You Become One*, and *An Actor Prepares . . . How to Work in New York City: How to Master the Business of the Business*. All three books reveal little-known secrets that make life much, much easier for the working performer. Wroe tells us how he came to educate other performers through his writing:

"I'm one of those people who, from the time I was cognizant of the work, wanted to be an actor. My mother tells me that as a child, I would sit in front of the TV and say, 'I wanna do that.' There was never anything else I wanted to do.

"I acted all the way through school. In high school, I got involved in musicals, and thought I wanted to be a musical comedy star. Then I went to college, at Loyola Marymount, and majored in political science—my family was always very against me being an actor, thinking I'd never make a living doing it. But I did have a theater minor, and I found I was spending more time in the theater department than in the political science department. I dropped political science after the first year for English. I went to Loyola Rome for a year, and took two Shakespeare classes—one in literature, and one was a directing Shakespeare class, taught by one of Peter Brook's associates. I thought I had died and gone to heaven; I thought Shakespeare was the greatest thing I'd ever discovered. I no longer wanted to be in musical theater, I wanted to be a Shakespearean actor.

"I decided to get my MFA in acting from a reputable school that focused on the classics, so I went to Catholic University in Washington, DC. Right out of there, I was asked to be in a production of *The Comedy of Errors* at the Folger Shakespeare Theater, which was sort of fulfilling my dream. I stayed on for two more years as a member of the company. It was a dream come true!

"At the end of my two years there, I decided it was time to move to New York City. Ever since I've been in New York, I've worked Off Broadway, in film, on television, and at several different leading regional theaters around the country. Eighteen, nineteen years of working continually went by. What I realized was that the one thing I'd done really well during those years besides being an actor was to live well in the city. All of my friends were envious at how well I'd lived on an actor's salary, and how I'd become so acclimated to the city, It got to the point where people where calling me literally every day to say, 'Hey, Craig, where can I find this?' or 'How can I do this inexpensively?'

"One day, in therapy, I was saying to my therapist how happy it made me that my friends thought I was this person to go to. He said, 'You know, Craig, I've always been amazed at how well you do here—you should think about writing a book.' I had never even thought about that, but I was an English major, and I'm a very good writer, I think—I love to write. So I thought, 'Oh, yeah!' The light bulb went off. I went home that night, and started compiling lists of ideas. After about two years, I had a file folder seven inches thick with my own notes, articles I'd cut out of the paper, things my friends had told me about.

"It was June 2001, and I didn't have a summer acting job. I thought, you know, I've got this big file sitting on my desk, and why don't I get to it? I sat down, and nine months later, I had my first book! When I wasn't doing a play, I could set my own hours, and I found I was writing fourteen, fifteen hours a day, literally. Or I was out in the field, doing research. I was loving it!

"The thing is, I didn't even try to sell my book before I had it finished. I'm really anal-retentive in the way that I can't focus on more than one thing, that I have to perfect one thing before I move on to the next. So I thought, I'll be trying to market the thing at the same time I'm trying to write it, so I made a pact with myself to write the entire thing, finish every single word, and then try to sell it.

"Once I'd finished it, I wrote a query letter during the summer of 2002, on a bus coming back from Cape Cod. I sent out letters at the end of that week to seven different publishing companies, and by the following Monday, I'd gotten phone calls from two different companies, telling me they wanted to publish my book. Just from the query letters and some sample chapters! I was completely confident about it. I was confident about my writing style, but more, I was confident about the material, that no one had ever written a book like this before. I just knew that people would want it; there was never a doubt in my mind. Ultimately, three different publishers wanted it; I was in a bidding war for about three months.

"A good chunk of that book is resources for actors, and one of them, I thought, would be the Actors' Work Program, which is a really wonderful thing. So I made an appointment to go to one of their Monday meetings. I wasn't looking for sideline work, because I worked constantly as an actor and acting teacher. I'd really gone to be an observer. But I was completely and totally mesmerized by Patch Schwadron, by her dedication to actors. I actually walked out of that meeting totally inspired by her, and I thought, this is a woman I need to get to know a little bit more, and I really need to know more about the Actors' Work Program.

"So I made an appointment to see Patch, sat down with her, and for a couple of hours, we just riffed. She pointed out so many things to me I hadn't thought about for my book. I really think that what they do is an amazing service.

"Everyone who reads my books who knows me says, 'My God, Craig, you so capture who you are in your writing. We get a clear, vivid sense of who you are.' I think if I weren't an actor, it would be more of a Fodor's guide, but I trusted myself enough to go, 'I've got to draw on myself in my life experiences as an actor, and I'm going to do the same thing in my writing.' I think that's why the first book was so successful, and spawned a second and third.

"I learned one big lesson in the twenty-one years I've lived in New York City: we are not defined by what we do. I really believe we are defined by who we love, and how we love. Work puts a roof over our heads, so that we can love.

"First and foremost, I'm an actor more than a writer. Here's a day as an actor-writer. I have auditions almost every day—sometimes I'll go on three commercial auditions a day, or a print go-see. When I was really in the throes of writing the book, I'd write from six to nine in the morning.

"At nine o'clock, I'd open my door and get my *New York Times*—I feel it's very important to stay in touch with the world. Then I'd set out on my auditions. Between auditions, I'd make a list of research places, because in my books, there's not a single place I haven't been to, experienced, or had firsthand knowledge of. I would then go sit in a Starbucks and jot down notes after I'd been to a few stores, or museums. I'd be also working around my private teaching schedule—I teach two nights a week. At the end of the day, about 7:00 or 8:00 PM, if I wasn't teaching, I'd sit down at my computer with my notes from the day and start writing again. I'd be writing till about one or two in the morning, sleep for four hours, and get up to do it all again.

"What I found was really important was creating some kind of a home office, where you've got your computer, your printer, a pencil sharpener. I'm on the tenth floor of a building, and I have a desk that looks out onto tennis courts and a playground, and see the Hudson and New Jersey, and I can't tell you how comforting that is. Like Virginia Woolf said: 'a room of one's own.' It's hard in New York to have a room of one's own, but it's easier to have a corner of one's own.

"If I can go to sleep saying, I was a good actor today, or I was a good writer today, that to me is success. Success is not in the achieving, it's in the striving for me."

seven
destinations and diversions

Careers in the recreational field can often be a perfect fit for an actor. You can really use your creative strengths to your advantage: first of all, there's a good chance you might actually be performing on a daily basis, such as with a cruise line, at a theme park, or via your own traveling act. You can also enjoy constant interaction with people, through guiding a tour, for example. Here's a secret, too—you might just find that if you create your own diversion-related job, you can actually rake in some big bucks.

The performers we cover in this chapter have all enjoyed steady, lucrative work traveling a number of different avenues. From an original, real-life member of the *Seinfeld* gang to an accomplished artist/businessman to a busy comic actor to a cruise line star to a rabbi-stand-up, you'll learn a lot—and enjoy the lessons.

THE STAR ATTRACTION

Kenny Kramer's life has been filled with adventure. He's been a successful stand-up comic, the manager of a popular British reggae band, the creator of a hot jewelry line—and oh, yes, he inspired a pop culture revolution. Kramer's good friend Larry David based the character of Kramer from the smash series *Seinfeld* on—you guessed it—Kramer. The rest is TV legend.

Since becoming an icon, Kramer has appeared on every TV show imaginable, chatting with Oprah Winfrey, mixing it up on *The Today Show*, getting profiled on *Dateline NBC*, CNN, MSNBC—he's even been a defendant on *Judge Judy*. The Libertarian Party made him their candidate for New York City mayor in 2001 (although Michael Bloomberg happened to win the election). Kramer didn't mind, though—he's got the tourism business to keep him plenty busy. For eleven sold-out years, Kramer has guided Big Apple visitors and residents on Kramer's Reality Tour, a fun and lively chance to visit the real-life locations the *Seinfeld* show made famous. The tour has been so successful, Kramer has taken it abroad: the Kramer Reality Road Show has been a smash hit overseas.

The warm and personable Kramer isn't simply gifted with a grand sense of humor; he's got intense business smarts. Listen to him explain how he's made it all happen:

"I started off as a drummer. I was going to the High School of Performing Arts; actually the school discouraged students from doing anything professionally while you were going to school. That didn't particularly appeal to me, so I found myself cutting school a lot to go to a café and watch people like Gene Krupa, Teddy Wilson, and Lionel Hampton do noon shows. I'd go out for lunch and not bother to come back. Gene Krupa befriended me; I became kind of a mascot there.

"At that time, you needed what was called a cabaret card to work in any place that sold liquor. At fifteen or sixteen, I lied about my age, got a fake birth certificate, got a cabaret card, and started playing jazz professionally. Then I got a job in the Catskill Mountains. I've got this gig up in a hotel in Parksville, where I'm making $150 a week to play six nights, and I have to do rehearsals. So I'm sitting there behind my drum set, and in walks this comedian who talks for an hour, picks up a check for $500 and then goes off to do a second show. I'd always been funny, like a class clown kind of a guy, and I realized, 'I'm in the wrong business.'

"Through a friend of a friend, I ended up getting a job as a chauffeur for a comedian named Jay Jayson, who was very popular in the Catskills. I used to drive Jay to his gigs, and carry in his wardrobe, and I started writing jokes for Jay. Jay is doing my jokes and they're getting great laughs, and I realize, hey, I could do these jokes myself. So on November 7, 1971, I stepped on a stage for the first time as a comedian, did my eight minutes that I created, tape-recorded it. It was a semi-disaster, but I learned a lot from it. So I went back again and again and again, and by December 31st of that year, I had my first professional work, booked for two shows on New Year's Eve—I'd started making a living as a stand-up comic.

"In 1972, I moved to Miami, and became one of the hot young comics there. All the comics in Miami were in their sixties and seventies, except for me for me and Gabe Kaplan. I befriended Gabe, and anywhere Gabe could work, I could work. So we kind of blazed a trail! So I'm entertaining these audiences in their fifties, sixties, seventies, and I'm doing OK, but I realized, I'm twenty-eight years old. If this is gonna be my fan base, by the time I'm in my forties, these people are gone. So I decided I needed to entertain my peers. In around '73 or '74, I started calling myself a 'rock comic'—I got friendly with some promoters, and started opening rock shows for Three Dog Night, the J. Geils Band, Ike and Tina Turner, Jose Feliciano. I did that for five or six years.

"Then I unexpectedly got custody of my daughter, who was five or six years old at the time. I could no longer live my life on the road—I had to be home. We settled in Miami—I'd put my daughter to bed at 8:00 PM, the babysitter would come, and I'd go do a 10:00 PM show somewhere. Next I got a gig in Philadelphia, doing a gig with the Flying Burrito Brothers. My daughter and I flew up together, and I let her spend a week with my mother in Teaneck, New Jersey, while I went down to the gig. As it turns out, there was this story when we were there in the *New York Times* about Manhattan Plaza, which was subsidized housing for performing artists just opening up. I canceled my flight the next day, went to take a look at the place, put in my application, my daughter and I got an apartment there, and I moved back to New York.

"This building was an amazing place—filled with performers, and everybody's on everybody else's demos, if you wrote a play you could get actors to do it, it was just terrific. By some bizarre circumstance, I just happened to come up with this idea for electronic jewelry. I started making a lot of money, like thousands of dollars a week, and I got really caught up in marketing this product that I made for nineteen cents and sold for $15.00. Nice profit margin! The jewelry business kind of took a toll on my stand-up. When agents would call me, where before I'd do shows for $350, $400, I'd raise my price to $2,500. After I told about four or five agents that was the only amount I'd work for, I was kind of out of show business. I'd lost the burn. In the beginning, it was very exciting, realizing my dream, but things came to the point where the amount of fun I was having was based on the amount of money I was making.

"While this was all happening, my friend Larry David, who also lived in Manhattan Plaza and who I'd met when I moved in, got a job on a TV show called *Fridays*, so he moved to LA. Then he wanted to move back to New York and asked me to help him find a place, so I finagled with the guy who lived across the hall from me to make Larry his roommate. That guy got a job on *Japanese Sesame Street*, so Larry lived there alone for five and a half years. One day, he comes into my apartment and says, 'Kramer, Jerry Seinfeld wants me to write this pilot with him, and I want to base a character on you.' Larry wrote the jokes—things that happened in real life, he turned into story lines on the show. Then Michael Richards did his own interpretation of what 'Kramer' was about. Michael is a terrific physical comedian, and that's his genius. The next thing you know, this is the biggest thing in the history of television. A character based on me is the most famous next-door neighbor since Ralph Kramden!

"I'm thinking, if I don't cash in on this, I'm a total idiot. CD-ROMs were very big at the time, and all of these publishers were opening up electronic media divisions. Since the character of Kramer is known as a guy who knows his way around, I came up with idea of doing a CD-ROM called *Kramer's New York: How to Live Like a Millionaire Without Spending Any Money. A Guide to New York*. I wrote a proposal, and started shopping it around, and heard the same thing over and over: basically what I was trying to do was sell a database, and if I really wanted a hit title, I needed either entertainment content or a game. So I'm thinking, what can I create, and I'm looking out my window, which faces 42nd Street. A Gray Line double-decker bus goes by, and a light bulb goes off in my head: 'A tour! I'm gonna do a tour!' Within ten minutes, I'm on the phone with the assistant to the president of Gray Line, setting up a meeting.

"I go in and I pitch them the idea—I want Gray Line to provide a bus for me to be the official transportation of the Kramer Reality Tour CD-ROM. The guy says, 'We'll be happy to do that for you, but why not actually do this tour, and we'll market it for you?' I had never thought of that. I wrote an itinerary, but basically Gray Line didn't work out, so I ended up renting my own theater and my own bus. The *New York Times* ran a big picture and story in the Metro section, above the fold, and the next day, there were film crews outside my door, up the yazoo—*Entertainment Tonight*, *Access Hollywood*, Reuters, AP. It was just amazing.

"I became media savvy, and a bit of a media slut, because I realized that it's much better to have publicity than pay for advertising. I've been able to nurture relationships with writers, and since *Seinfeld*'s a hit in ninety countries, there have been articles about me everywhere. On the tour, about 40 percent of the customers are international visitors—Australians, Brits, Germans, you name it. I got an e-mail from a guy in Australia who said, 'If you ever come to Australia, I have a large publicity company, and would love to do your PR.' I said, 'Well, get me a job in Australia—I'll turn my tour into a stage presentation.' He said, 'Ever done it before?' I said, 'No, but I know I can.' So based on my word that I could deliver a show, he spent a few hundred thousand dollars renting theaters and doing publicity. I went to Australia, the show was a huge, sold-out hit, and I've been back subsequently. In Australia, I'm like a superstar!

"Now I only do the tour about five months a year. I only do the tour once a week; I add Sundays on holiday weekends, because we were turning away so many people. I could be doing this every day, and I'd be making four or five thousand a day on it, but then it would be like having a job. Like, I'd get up in the morning and say, 'Ohhh, I've gotta do this.' But this way, I get up on Saturday mornings, and look forward to it. Plus, *Seinfeld* fans are the coolest people; they're basically smart, rich people with a sense of humor. If I'm gonna hang out with anybody, that's the type I'm hanging with! Every tour, the audiences are just so appreciative.

"My whole life, I just loved to make people laugh. It's like a mission from God. If there are people in my audience who've just lost a loved one, or have cancer, if you've got them laughing, there's no pain. There's just joy. That's always been my calling, and has evolved through everything I do.

"I read this somewhere, but it's so true: if you just find something you love to do, and make that your work, you'll never work a day in your life. I love my life. I love the fact that I'm able to do what I want to do."

MY WAY

Paul Salos entered show business over fifty years ago, and his performance talent has earned him many wonderful honors and once-in-a-lifetime experiences. He's sung with Count Basie; appeared on the TV hit *Walker, Texas Ranger*; and made two concert tours of the Far East. His greatest joy as a singer/actor, however, is interpreting the work of his idol, Frank Sinatra. Salos has performed a Sinatra tribute show at special events all over the world; he was especially thrilled to do the show at Caesars Palace, Sinatra's own signature performance spot. His spot-on sound-a-like talents can also be heard on his hit CD, *Salos Sings Sinatra: The Magic of Sinatra Lives*.

Salos has become one of the cruise industry's most popular attractions as well. Such work may look easy to get and easy to do, but Salos will be the first to tell you the true score. Here, he discusses the rules he uses to maintain his business and art, and offers very wise advice for young performers hoping to follow him into cruise line work.

Rule #1: Develop Your Skill Set Beyond Reproach

"Going back to when I was fifteen to eighteen years old, I developed impressions of people like Al Jolson, Jimmy Durante, and Alfred Hitchcock. I then moved on to master Perry Como, Jerry Lewis, Dean Martin. And finally—Frank Sinatra.

"I grew up within eight or nine miles from where Mr. Sinatra did in Hoboken. Everything he got, he fought for, just like I did. I loved the way he performed, his ballads. Tommy Dorsey gave him his start, and as a young performer, he worked hard—he actually broke his vocal cord. He was an inspiration, and once I built my skills doing singing impressions, I set out to add him to my repertoire. It wasn't easy, though—during his career, every two years, his voice kept changing, from his sound as a young kid to his more mature voice. Yet my name, Paul, means 'many gifts' in Greek, and I eventually accomplished the impression."

Rule #2: Cruise Work Is Tough, So Be Up to the Challenge

"In approaching a cruise line for entertainment work, you've got to have a performance DVD or video, and a CD—you must come prepared as a total professional. Cruise lines generally look for family-oriented entertainment: comics, magicians, singers, variety acts. Because I was an impressionist, they liked me immediately.

"It's not an easy job, though. Performers are usually required to do ship duties as well as their show work. This means, you do a show that ends past midnight, and then you've got to get up at 7:30, go down to the gangplank, and count passengers. Or you may be on call to announce numbers at bingo games! At this point, I personally have nearly worked my way up to assistant cruise director.

"The benefit, though, is when the crowds like you. Then you get rebooked, and you get more money the next time. Cruise lines usually want a three to six month commitment per booking from a performer."

Rule #3: Do Your Best and Then Some

"I hone my craft to perfection. You just can't go out and do a mediocre show. Give your audience 125 percent, and expect 75 percent back. Most performers don't think like that. Also, I prepare meticulously for my shows. I never eat after 2:00 PM; I vocalize as much as possible to get that rubber band loosened up, get my vocal cords going. My tools for success are the following: know your craft; be the best you can be; have great promo material; have good ethics; have great professionalism; always be well-groomed; don't burn bridges; and always give everything you've got to your audience, whether that audience numbers one person or one hundred."

AN UNORTHODOX CAREER

Bob Alper enjoys two prosperous dual careers—both good for the soul. He's a wildly popular stand-up comic whose gigs take him to clubs and college campuses all over America. He's also a practicing rabbi, who you can find conducting High Holiday services in Buffalo and Philadelphia.

Sure, combining these positions may seem like quite the conflict of interest, but Alper's success proves otherwise. He's been featured on Showtime, *Good Morning, America*, CNN, and the BBC. In his own words, he tells how his professional life fell into place, and why he wouldn't trade this work for the world:

"I was ordained in 1972, and became assistant rabbi at a huge synagogue in Buffalo. I was there for six years; in 1978, I went on to have what's called a solo pulpit, with my own congregation, around 450 families, in the Philadelphia suburbs. I did that for eight years; I was pretty successful, I thought, but also, was not delighted. So after fourteen years, I'd earned a ministry doctorate degree, and with that, I decided to leave congregation life and do rabbinical functions, like weddings and funerals, plus open a counseling practice.

"I got as far as sharing an office with a psychiatrist, and then comedy reared its ugly head in the summer of 1986. I entered the Jewish Comic of the Year contest in Philadelphia. Comedy had always been a passion and a hobby in my life, but had not really been a dream, because of the impossibility of it—I thought I'd never be able to BE a comedian. But anyway, I entered this contest, and came in third behind a chiropractor and a lawyer. Fortunately, though, one of the judges was the host of *A.M. PHILADELPHIA*, the top-rated local TV morning show. She thought I should have won; I agreed with her. So she had me on the show, both as a guest, and filmed doing stand-up at a club. I went back to the same place the contest had been held, Goin' Bananas, and did a longer set, maybe fifteen minutes. After I was done, the owner of this club took me aside and gave me $25. He was more ceremonial about it than I was—'This is your first comedy pay, and you'll remember it.' I shrugged, 'Thanks'—but I remember it.

"I started to do a lot of open mikes, then started charging to do private shows. My business kept growing and growing. I've been more successful every year—the number of shows I do rises, the fees rise, my income rises, and that's a way to measure success. Also, things started to happen that I never expected. In 2005, for the first time, I worked with Ahmed Ahmed, an Arab Muslim comic who's known for his work with Vince Vaughn; about 40 percent of my shows now are with Ahmed. We've got two promoters renting theaters for us.

"For me, it's a very nice combination of living in rural Vermont, and then going to various cities to do comedy—a nice kind of back-and-forth. I think if I lived in a big city, then went to big cities, it wouldn't be a thrill. I like traveling. I like nice hotels, room service, stuff like that. My wife comes with me when I do a show somewhere like Puerto Rico.

"On the road, here's a typical day: I take a morning flight, say, to Cleveland. Ahmed will be flying in from Chicago, so we'll meet at the airport. We'll take a rented car and drive for about an hour and a half to the venue. Then we take the afternoon to prepare for the show. I'll take a nap, have a nice dinner, then do a sound check, hang around, do the show, which is the best part, drive to the airport again the next morning, and go home. It's pretty easy. The only downside at some shows is, some old Jewish man will come up and start telling me jokes. 'You can use this, Rabbi.' 84 percent of the jokes old Jewish men tell me contain the world 'penis,' so I kinda steer clear. But that's part of the game.

"You meet all kinds of people. Ahmed and I were at a bar in Boise, Idaho—I never go to bars, except when I travel. This Boise guy, a little drunk, comes up to Ahmed and says, 'What are you doing here?' Ahmed says, 'I'm a comedian.' The guy says, 'Where ya performin', the Funny Bone?' Ahmed says, 'No, at the synagogue.' The guy asks, 'You a Jew?' and Ahmed says, 'No, I'm an Arab,' and the guy says, 'Jews, Arabs, same thing. What are ya doin' tomorrow?' Ahmed says, 'I don't know, just hangin' out.' The guy asks, 'Wanna go shoot squirrels? We go about fifty miles outside of town, shoot ground squirrels, and eat 'em.' Ahmed turned him down because, he said, 'I didn't want anybody to pick up the paper the next morning and read DEAD ARAB FOUND NEXT TO WOUNDED SQUIRREL.'

"Ahmed and I have developed a lot of material together. We get paid nicely, but there's so much more to it. We did a show at the University of Pennsylvania, and there were Muslim women wearing hijabe, and Jewish students wearing yarmulkes, sitting side by side socializing, having a great time, laughing. My line is, 'You can't hate someone with whom you've laughed.' So there's that peacemaking, a lot of ramifications we hadn't anticipated, and it's very rewarding.

"I was doing a show, and afterwards a woman came up to me to say, 'Rabbi, six months ago my husband died, and this is the first time I've laughed.' I was also told about a woman who had cancer.

When she and her husband went to her chemotherapy, they took my comedy tape with them, and listened on earphones. A woman also reported to me that she brought a friend of hers to one of my shows, and her friend was dying of cancer. Her friend turned to her afterwards and said, 'You know, for an hour and a half, I forgot I was sick.' You can't beat those kinds of rewarding responses.

"Comedy is something from which you can never retire. Bob Newhart had a great line; when somebody asked him at age seventy-five why he still continued to do stand-up, he replied, 'It's worth having to take my shoes off at the airport to make people laugh.' You keep on doing it, because it's something you love doing."

TO BE THE BEST

Sean Cercone has a deep commitment to quality, and it shows. Cercone is vice president and artistic director of the Carousel Dinner Theatre in Akron, Ohio, the world's largest professional dinner theater. Chosen as one of *Crain's Business* 40 Under 40 Top Executives of 2004, Cercone's sharp-as-a-tack business sensibility, paired with his accomplished acting background, is a major tool the Carousel organization has used to innovate its programming and establishment. Cercone explains how he got to his lofty position, and the strategies he employs to keep Carousel one of the country's top theatrical tourist destinations:

"I come from an artistic family. My dad was a hippie, traveled around the country in a magic school bus playing bluegrass music. My mom is a visual artist/painter; I was a child born out of that. A very liberal, open, artistic home, with musical instruments all over the place.

"My interest in theater really started to take hold when I was about thirteen. I won tickets to see a Broadway play called *Checkmates*. It starrred Paul Winfield, Ruby Dee, and Denzel Washington. Denzel's stage work was phenomenal. To this day, I remember specific physical actions that he used that were so amazing and poignant. I was fascinated by that guy—he was so influential, in those two hours of my life, on me, and what I found I wanted to do, too.

"My parents were pushing me into the medical field, though—they were like, 'You could be a nurse and do your acting thing on the side.' That just did not work out, though. I failed out of a bunch of colleges, and I just said, OK, if I'm gonna do acting, I'm gonna do this by myself. I put myself through Frostberg State University in western Maryland, which had a very low ratio of actors to teachers, and that was great. Then at my MFA training program at West Virginia University, spending the years there studying, breaking through my frustrations as an actor, learning how to break down and approach a character—it was all VERY vital.

"In a theory and thesis class I had, our final paper asked us how we would develop a professional Equity theater as part of the school's theater program. Word of my paper somehow got out; I got a phone call from a gentleman at a state park in Fairmount, West Virginia, who said, 'I like your idea. I have $12,000 to provide you guys if you're interested in developing a festival here in the summertime.' Of course, this was a great opportunity. I researched tax Web sites, government Web sites, without a lawyer, and I created the West Virginia Shakespeare Festival as a not-for-profit organization.

"That was a major turning point. I was really fascinated by putting a show together. As an actor, I'd always find myself focused on what a SHOW meant as opposed to just focusing on my role. After graduation, my wife and I moved to New York City, and I was auditioning and waiting tables, and nothing was happening. I wasn't Equity, I couldn't get into Equity auditions, and it was a tough slog. I decided to look for a more steady income, and my wife really didn't like New York. There was a position open here at the Carousel Dinner Theatre as an assistant to the producer. As I'd produced the festival, I thought I could learn a lot about running a successful business. When I came out to interview, I realized that this organization, despite having a thirty-year history at the time, was really in its infancy artistically. New owners had bought the theater, and their goal was to increase artistic quality.

"I had never been to a dinner theater, so I expected actors serving food; that is not the case. We are an $8 million company, with a $2.4 million production budget and thirteen Equity contracts per show—we cast all of our shows out of New York. What I saw was an infrastructure that had so much potential, with the right kind of leadership it would be able to blossom into an amazing regional theater. So we moved to Akron, Ohio—it was only about eight days from when they made me the offer to when we arrived. Then, I became artistic director at the age of twenty-nine—really young for the job!

"With great entrepreneurial spirit, our owner, Joe Palmer, said, 'I'm open to whatever.' But I have to hit my budget, and I have to make sure that we're hitting x amount of people per year. That was an environment I understood, and I could see us pushing and pulling back and forth to do things for our audience. Artistically, there are things that don't cost any money that we are able to do in the concept of a production that just wows our audience. They've never seen an approach to a production in that way. For instance, Joe really pushed for us to do *Urinetown*, which is a huge risk—very few theaters in the country are producing it at this time.

"As a leader, you've got to foster cooperative, collaborative relationships. You have to be open. As soon as you say, it's my way or the highway, you've closed yourself off to options and opportunities you wouldn't think of. You are not the ultimate God of Theater. What's really great about the team we've put together is exceptional; they all have a passionate love for what they do, and that benefits this organization. We do extremely important work; we're on the front line of cultural/social issues in our work here, especially in Middle America, in red state/blue state Ohio, where the battle is being fought every day.

"I wake up every single day and thank God I have the job I have. I'm doing what I love to do, even when it's a sixteen, eighteen-hour day. I could do it standing on my head, because I love what I do. To me, this is success. Everything over and above this for the rest of my career is gravy!"

THE GOOD GUY

Gil Christner's generosity is as big as his jam-packed resume. This popular comic actor has appeared on tons of sitcoms, from *The Bernie Mac Show* to *3rd Rock from the Sun*; on TV dramas like *The West Wing* and *Buffy the Vampire Slayer*; and in films like *Mystery Men*. Equally impressive is his desire to use his past experiences to help newcomers grab a foothold in the business he loves so much.

One of Christner's early gigs involved working at Disneyland. He shares his war stories from the Mouse House, his admiration for those who taught HIM the ropes, and his sage advice on how to navigate a career with equal doses of vision and optimism.

Disneyland Confidential

"It was really quite fun! I auditioned kind of on the urging of my wife—there was heavy singing and dancing around, and I'm a terrible singer and dancer. But I'm very funny, and luckily the part I tried out for was the comic relief, Sam the Bartender. Twenty-five years previous to my show, they had one specific show that was basic vaudeville, dressing in western gear and stuff like that. Then some new people took over the administration at Disneyland, and the people who had been working in that show for twenty-five years all got fired. The show I got into replaced theirs, which I didn't know until I got there and we got all sorts of nasty letters from other employees: 'My friend's out on his can because of you guys!' I was just trying to get a job!

"It was great times. I really enjoyed the thrill of working at Disneyland, and also the thrill of seeing the backstage secrets of Disneyland. Like, now I could take you to Disneyland and show you the secret passageways and underground places. You may not know this, but there's a huge employee cafeteria under the restaurant in Pirates of the Caribbean!

"The thing about this new show was that it actually had a little bit of a plot. So I was Sam the Bartender, and my old flame Miss Lily came to town, and some other cowboy came in and tried to take her away from me. It was a strictly G-rated show. There was one line about a 'chest of drawers,' comparing Miss Lily and the dancing girls to furniture. I did a vaudeville move where I just kind of thrust out my hips while the drummer made a rimshot. The people in charge took me aside and said, 'Can't do that. This is a family show.' So their standards are very, very strict, and you know, you can't blame them. They've got a formula, and it works, and I love Disneyland.

"I did something else that I was not supposed to do. We did six shows a day, and in between shows, you had about an hour to an hour and a half to hang out. You're not supposed to go on the rides, but I always did. I went on Space Mountain six times in a row one time."

Make Your Own Luck

"It never occurred to me that other people weren't versatile. I'd show up on some set, and I'd have a script I was working on.

People would say, 'Oh! You write?' I'd say, 'Yeah, this is for a radio gig I do.' 'Oh! You're in radio?' I'd think, 'Gee, you're in show business, why aren't you doing a hundred things?' I would really suggest to people starting out: try to do as many things in the business as you can. I would recommend if you have to get a day job to pay the bills, try to get a day job somewhere in the business, doing something that's oriented toward what you ultimately want to do.

"I always believed success was possible. As I kept striving to be a success, I realized one day, I've been making a living at this—I guess I'm a success. There's an old saying in this old cowboy philosopher's book I saw that says, 'One day, if you wake up and find you're a success, you probably haven't been asleep.' I think that's true, because I was willing to take these different jobs to supplement my income, to make sure I could stay alive and stay in Los Angeles.

"I'm not a real New Age kinda guy, but I am a real firm believer in energy. The universe is pretty much built on energy, and physics is pretty much how we live, so I believe that if you put some new energy into your work, your life, and your goals, if nothing else, you're not gonna be sitting home crying. You're gonna be getting things done. There are a few things I've learned over the years, and one of them is, something that you do today may not pay off today, and it may not pay off next week, but it could pay off five years from now."

eight
the communications connection

It's a Golden Rule: if you want to work professionally as an actor, you've got to present a polished and total package. In today's hyper-commercial entertainment industry, without great vocal technique, strong people skills, and a marketable look, you will be ignored by agents and producers, even if you can perform circles around the ghost of Olivier. So it's no wonder that most working actors hone their personal presentation very, very carefully: studying voice, amping up the old personality, and developing strong personal style. Really, it's all about having that knack for good communication: whether you're verbalizing or simply walking into a room, you want to put your best foot forward in terms of the message you're sending.

This kind of communication savvy is also absolutely essential when an actor decides to turn his or her attention to pursuing an alternate career path. The actors we're about to meet in this chapter have very smartly taken the tricks they've learned while developing image tools and parlayed them into consistent, highly successful livings. Here's how they made it happen.

THE VOICE MASTER

You've seen Bob Bergen on-camera in scores of series like *The Facts of Life*, *Gimme a Break*, and *Days of Our Lives*. He's also been a game show host, grandstand host of the annual Hollywood Christmas Parade, and the star of his own one-man show, with which he's opened concert tours for Kenny Rogers. Bergen's career track detours from many other heavily employed actors, however, in that he is literally living his dream through an alternate career: he's the voice of Porky Pig (not to mention many other animated characters including Tweety Bird, Speedy Gonzales, Marvin the Martian, and Sylvester, Jr.). Bergen's not only voiced these characters on TV, he's also lent his talents to films like *Space Jam* and *Gremlins*.

This affable pro addresses how he maneuvered his gift for breathing life into a cartoon character into a lucrative lifestyle—and imparts his bold, go-for-it job philosophy.

Staking His Claim

"When I was five, I told my parents when I grew up, I wanted to be Porky Pig. My mom said, 'You can't be Porky Pig—you're Jewish.' All I knew was, I had watched cartoons and fallen in love with this little stuttering pig. My parents bought me a tape recorder for my birthday, and I'd keep it by the TV to daily record cartoons. I figured out there was one guy, Mel Blanc, doing every voice in all of these cartoons, and I started deciphering his formula. Instinctively, I knew there was more to it than just doing a voice—it's capturing the whole persona. I'd study character's facial expressions, inflections—I would practice doing characters constantly.

"We moved to Los Angeles when I was fourteen. I thought, the first thing I should do is call Mel Blanc to ask, when can I do what you do? I didn't even know that was a rude or inappropriate thing to do. My dad went around town and got me every phone book, from

Beverly Hills to the west end of the Valley, but I couldn't find Mel Blanc. But there was a show on years back called *Wonderama*, and Mel Blanc was a guest on that, and he'd mentioned his wife's name was Estelle. So I tried her name, and found her in the Pacific Palisades phone book.

"I called, and talked to Mel. I asked him questions, like how did he do it, how did he get an agent, and he told me his story, which didn't relate to me, because he'd started in the thirties, a very different time. I asked him if he still did cartoons, and he said he hadn't done them in years, he was doing commercials and was currently doing voice-over for *Looney Tunes on Ice*, for Warner Brothers. So I called the studio, and I said, 'I'm calling to confirm Mel Blanc's appointment this Thursday at nine.' They said, 'We have him on the books for Wednesday at eleven,' and I said, 'You know what, you're right, my mistake, I put in the wrong date, so sorry.' I told my mom, 'Wednesday I'm skipping school, and you're gonna take me to watch Mel Blanc work.'

"When we got to the studio, I told the receptionist we were guests of Mel Blanc, and when we walked into the booth I told the producer we were friends of the receptionist. I sat and watched him work; for me, it was as close to any religious experience I'd ever had. In one hand, he had a cigarette and in the other he had oxygen. He would take a puff on the cigarette, and then take a puff of oxygen, and did the character. I watched his body language and facial expressions, and I realized you're not just doing voices, you're performing from head to toe.

"About this same time, I called Hanna Barbera, and they referred me to Daws Butler, who was every voice Mel Blanc wasn't— Yogi Bear, Huckleberry Hound, Captain Crunch, Elroy Jetson, Snagglepuss. I got into Daws's workshop, and also studied with anybody who offered a voiceover class. They wouldn't hire kids back then, but a few years later, Casey Kasem, who shared a mutual friend with my family, sent me his headshot as a high school graduation present. I sent him a note: 'Dear Casey Kasem, thank you for the head shot, can I have your job?' I put my phone number down. He called me up, and asked, 'Do you have a demo? Are you union? Do you have an agent?' After four years of workshops, nobody had ever mentioned the words 'demo,' 'union,' or 'agent' to me. You can be the world's greatest actor, but without the business smarts, none of it matters.

"Casey said, 'Make me a homemade demo.' He gave it to his agent, and the agent decided to represent me. Now, my cousin had taken me to a party with her when I was sixteen, where I'd met a bank teller who I told I wanted to be Porky. The bank teller called up out of the blue around the same time and said, 'If you still want to do cartoons, I might have a job for you. To make a long story short, I've now become the head of talent for Marvel Productions.' I went to Marvel and auditioned for a new cartoon, *Spider Man and His Amazing Friends*. I booked it, I got my SAG card, and my agent was happy, because he hadn't had to lift a finger.

"Things have changed a bit since I did this. Nowadays, nobody's gonna make a homemade demo tape and expect an agent to listen—it's gotten too competitive. One real important tip would be, don't pursue voice-over till you're ready. There's only about fifteen voice-over agents in LA, and they have your type already. Be tenacious and passionate. Don't give a damn about the competition—you're the only you reading for the part. Jimmy Stewart was Jimmy Stewart in everything he did. Cagney was Cagney. Tom Hanks is always Tom Hanks."

The Big Break

"In 1989, Mel Blanc died. I heard it on the radio while I was driving down Wilshire Boulevard, and had two emotions: 'Oh, my God, my hero died,' and 'Oh, my God, what does this mean for me?' Mel had gone on a two-year publicity tour with his son, saying 'My son's gonna take over when I go,' so to this day, people think his son does his voices! But they started holding auditions for the Looney Tunes characters. Mel's son had already recorded for *Tiny 'Toons*, but then they decided, well, he's not exactly right for Porky. Plus, he was in a helicopter crash with Kirk Douglas, so he wasn't available. They called me in and said, 'We need you to replace him as Porky, plus do Tweety Bird.' I said 'GREAT!'

"Usually, you record voices first, and they animate to the sound-track. But the first job I did as Porky, I had to watch the cartoon and dub in my voice. His voice was different and he stuttered differently, so it wasn't the world's greatest performance—I was a little concerned I was gonna look bad. But they called me in again and again and again.

"I remember when I got Porky Pig, my parents took me out to dinner. As soon as I sat down, I got this wave of depression.

My mom asked, 'Are you OK?' I said, 'You know, I'm only in my early twenties, and I've reached my lifelong goal. What do I do for the rest of my life?' My mom said, 'Worry about that as your life goes on.' "

All in a Day's Work

"I've had my most heartfelt, I-wanna-get-outta-this-business moments during my most successful times. I'll be doing something I'm not passionate about; it's a JOB. I've worked for directors and thought, 'This is not a nice person. This person is not fun to be with.' So I'll say to my agent, 'You know what? I think I'll pass on that director's next project.' I'm not gonna sacrifice my integrity and my dignity for a paycheck. There will be more paychecks. Life is too short.

"Voice-over is very different than on-camera television work, because there's no hiatus—there's always work to be had. Everything's a cold read, and you audition in your agent's office— they all have studios. My agent will call and say, 'Can you come in at eleven?' but I always get there at 10:30 so I have time to prepare. I might have twenty scripts—five TV commercials, five radio commercials, five animated characters, five CD-ROM games, etc. In thirty minutes, I have to have established characters prepared and ready to go."

Tricks of the Trade

"Improv training is essential, because it makes you think fast on your feet. I teach an animation voice-over class and cover real specific techniques to create the character. With experience, those techniques become second nature. For me, what solidified my ability to make fast choices was when I started re-voicing actors in movies. I started auditioning for looping jobs, taking the dirty words out for the TV version of a movie. You only come in at the last half of the line! I re-voiced Leonardo DiCaprio in *The Basketball Diaries*, but only when he was on heroin—another actor dubbed him when he played sober. He was having a crying fit, and I had to be in the moment, vocally right, and my acting had to match his in the middle of a line! Doing that over and over again absolutely trained me in cold reading.

"I was working before I really studied acting. I'm now a Meisner-trained actor, and once I found that foundation for my talent, and could make specific choices and know WHY I was making them, it all fit together, like pieces of a puzzle.

"About four or five years ago, I put together a once-a-month happy hour called Vox on the Rocks, for anybody in the world of voice-over. It's not necessarily a place you wanna pass out your demos, but it's a way to socially meet really nice people, so if you do send your demo to them, or meet them at an audition, there's a connection. And not a desperate, please-hire-me connection."

Seal of Approval

"I met Jim Henson once in person, when I was working on his show *Fraggle Rock*. He would send notes, and then the producers took me to the Broadcast Museum's *An Evening With Jim Henson*. He had Kermit with him, and Kermit was looking around, alive, the whole time Jim was talking to people. Jim's natural voice was Kermit, and he said, 'You're Wembley on *Fraggle Rock*. I think you're very good.' And I said, 'I think YOU'RE very good!' That's the icing on the cake in this business."

Sage Advice

"Enjoy the journey! The journey never ends. If the journey puts a smile on your face, that's success. If disappointment makes you go, 'now I've got a challenge,' that to me is success. You've got to enjoy the road, bumps and all."

INSPIRED INTERPRETATION

Laura Giannelli has graced prestigious stages all over the Washington DC area, from Arena to the Source Theatre to the Kennedy Center. Roles in *The Memory of Water* and *The Wayward Man* and *The Rapture* earned her the distinguished Mary Goldwater award as well. Giannelli finds her work as a book-on-tape narrator just as rewarding as these immense theatrical achievements, however. To date, she has recorded over 650 books, and has lectured on this craft for the Library of Congress. Giannelli gives us an illuminating glimpse inside the way she interprets the printed word.

Q: How and why did you first choose to pursue acting?

A: I first fell in love with theater playing "let's pretend" with my mother and younger sister when I was about four or five years old. My mother grew up in New York City, going to opera and theater as a girl, so she always talked passionately about the power of performance to change the world. As I grew older and started school, I really responded whenever we did role-playing or small performances at school. Fast-forward to the tenth grade, while my family was living in Wiesbaden, Germany—my dad was in the Air Force. I was cast in two plays that solidified my love of theater and acting: I played Rebecca Nurse in *The Crucible* at the ripe old age of fifteen, and still remember loving how quiet the crowd got when I spoke. And I played the cranky spinster in *Ten Little Indians*; the audience HISSED my character! I was really beginning to feel the power of communicating with an audience.

Once I was accepted at the Catholic University of America in Washington, DC, and began to really study my craft, there was really no looking back. One of my drama teachers there, Bill Graham, Sr., said something that has stayed with me always. He told us that if there was anything else we thought we could be happy doing for a living, we should do that instead of acting. Theater is such a difficult and demanding profession, he said, that one should only commit to it if one was really, really certain that no other life's work would do. That made sense to me; I knew I was really sure acting was what I wanted to do with my life.

Q: How did you further diversify by becoming a books-on-tape artist?

A: When I was first out of college, I was not getting a lot of stage work. I worked for a couple of summers in the box office at Olney Theatre in Olney, Maryland. One of the fellows I got to know there complimented my voice and said I ought to consider doing talking books for the Library of Congress's National Library Service for the Blind and Physically Handicapped. He'd begun working there as a grad student and was about to leave the job, so he knew there would be at least one opening. Using his name, I called for an audition. The wheels turned slowly, as they tend to do in government, but a year and a half later, I started working at the recording studio, first as an engineer (what we call a monitor), and finally, almost a year after that, as a narrator. It's really a very logical job for an actor! Reading books aloud was right up my alley.

Branching out into doing the occasional commercial or industrial narration in addition to my talking book work was just a matter of referrals from people who knew I narrated books. Then, once I got one job, another would come along. Also, I'm on file with the local casting agencies that know I do voice work, and I get calls from time to time from them for voiceover or other industrial or commercial jobs.

Incidentally, there are a lot of actors in the Washington, DC area who narrate books as their non-acting, pay-the-rent job. In addition to the Library of Congress's in-house studio, there is also a commercial house here (Potomac Talking Book Services) that subcontracts with the Library to record NLS books. A number of other narrators who record in a converted closet or basement studio in their own homes for commercial outlets like Blackstone Audio Books or Books on Tape, based in Oregon and California, respectively.

Q: How do you specifically employ your acting skills in books-on-tape work?

A: To me, narrating a talking book is just as fully an acting job as playing a role onstage. I just get to play ALL the parts, instead of only one. I have an image in my head for each of the characters in a novel as I read. I SEE the scene in my head as I "play" it with my voice. When I prepare to narrate a book, I also think of myself as standing in for the author, be the book fiction or non-fiction. I am telling "my" story to the listener, and I try to have the same commitment to the material as if I had written it myself. Rather the same way an actor must commit to his/her character in a play, giving 100 percent to bringing that character to life for an audience.

In addition, as a narrator I use a lot of what I learned in college about voice production and articulation, pitch control, etc. The talking book listener has to be able to clearly understand what a narrator is saying, and to be able to distinguish between narration and dialogue, as well as between the two or more people having a conversation in that dialogue. If the listener can't understand you, none of your carefully created characters will mean a thing.

Q: What is your proudest career accomplishment thus far?

A: I believe my proudest career accomplishment so far has been winning the Alexander Scourby Narrator of the Year Award for Children's Literature back in 1990. The award is given each year by the American Foundation for the Blind in New York, and back when I won the award, it was sort of a 'People's Choice'—a committee of young talking book listeners, blind children, who picked ME as their favorite!"

SOPHISTICATED LADY

Samantha von Sperling's innate sense of flair, style, and culture served her tremendously well when it came to cutting a glamorous figure as a dancer/actress on film, Off Broadway, and in many a music video. Her life hasn't been a bed of roses, however; a series of tough personal and professional challenges forced her to start over in an entirely new business. The good news? Her fresh venture, the Manhattan- and Boston-based image consulting firm Polished Information, is a smash hit. This chic survivor relates how she persevered through hardship to find her true calling—helping others improve their own lives:

"I'm originally from Boston—my mother's French, my father's British. I'm somewhat the oddball, in the sense that even though artistic endeavors were accepted in my family, I was the only performing artist. My father is a renowned psychiatrist; everybody else is a dress designer, industrial designer, architect. So an artistic endeavor is acceptable as long as you are successful at it.

"I always kind of just knew who I was—as I kid, I took tap, jazz, did all the school plays. When I got to high school, I joined the drama club, did talent shows, joined the jazz choir and the gospel choir. I knew that I liked to dance, but it never dawned on me to do it professionally. I had professors at NYU lament that I didn't start ballet at five, because I had perfect feet—one said, 'Your arches were wasted on you!' I didn't even start dancing competitively until I was eighteen, which is very late for someone who went on to dance professionally.

"I KNEW I was going to go to NYU, and I did. I was a little too frightened at that time to audition for Tisch, but I started out as a public relations major, then switched to their educational theater department. I took as many dance classes as they would allow, and at

113

that time, you could also take private voice classes as a full-credit course. So I basically took private opera classes for four years, which was great—I felt it was a tremendous gift. I took all the dance, voice, acting, and singing I could get my hands on. I also started out as mascot of NYU's ballroom dance team, and one year later, was its captain. We won a lot of competitions while I was on the team.

"When I graduated from college, I went to work as a dance instructor at Arthur Murray—they were thrilled to have me because they didn't have to train me. But I didn't get paid enough, and I thought, I can do this by myself! I guess the beauty of being young and naive is that you don't know what you don't know, and that allows you to do crazy, ridiculous things. So I sold all of my furniture, because I lived in a doorman building with wood floors, and that was all I needed. I had a friend who magically made some mirrors fall off a truck, and I had wall-to-wall mirrors! A few clients followed me from Arthur Murray, and I placed a teeny tiny little ad in *New York Wedding Magazine*, not to mention the fact that I hustled clients every night at every dance spot. And so I had a successful dance studio in Manhattan! I only taught private lessons, taught financial types and Wall Street types, so I taught them in the evening and had the flexibility to audition in the daytime.

"I got a lot of work as a dancer in film. I did movies like *Carlito's Way*, *Curtain Call*, and *Woo*. I had a couple agents; I collaborated with a lot of fellow artists. Then one day there were music videos to do, and I was choreographing. I managed to make a very steady living using my performance skills; I didn't have to waitress, or change air conditioner filters in a dance studio, which was an actual job I had when I was starting out! It was very empowering knowing I could pursue my dream without having to work at a desk 9:00 AM to 5:00 PM.

"Somewhere around 1998, I could feel I was getting really close to my big break. I was working with enough people in the big leagues that I was getting there. The Olympics were going to include ballroom dancing as a sport, and I was at the top of my game, so it was going to be my chance. Then, tragically, I woke up one morning, and I couldn't walk. It had happened before; I had strained my lateral collateral ligament. I'd gotten steroid injections in my knees, which held me over for a year. But between dancing, training, teaching, and auditioning, I'd worn away my meniscus in both knees, and frayed both lateral collateral ligaments. I went to

Boston, saw two of the most famous orthopedic surgeons on the East Coast. One of them said, 'If you don't want to walk with a cane by the time you're thirty, you need to understand that you're now a retired racehorse.'

"It took me years to get over that; I was crushed. My boyfriend said, 'I'm moving to New Caanan, Connecticut, to the suburbs; come with me and be a Stepford Wife.' I started to rationalize that I'd had my fantasy life and I should face up to reality, do what 'normal' people do. I didn't last nine months. I was so depressed and fat! The Wagon Wheel Committee with its matching blondes in twinsets, I couldn't deal, I couldn't relate! The relationship collapsed, and I found myself homeless, penniless, jobless—it was very scary.

"I really didn't know what to do. I went back to Manhattan, slept on couches till I ran out of sofas. I just couldn't get it together, couldn't figure out a game plan. Then I moved to the south to do telecommunications, and THAT was a horrible disaster. I lasted eighteen months, then went to Boston in 1999, back to my family, with my tail between my legs. It was literally that or the street. I thought, all right, maybe I'm NOT supposed to have the fabulous life I dreamed for myself. Let me just get through this and see what happens. I kind of needed some time to heal. Within nine days, I'd gotten an apartment two blocks from my mother's house, a little studio in the Back Bay, which had good karma. I needed a job immediately, but who was gonna hire an out-of-work actress who'd failed at telecommunications?

"So what I did was go to work at the Lancome cosmetics counter at Filene's. I had worked as a make-up artist between dancing, had taken classes in theater, film, and TV make-up in college. I quickly learned that I really hated working for a department store, so I left, and was helping my mother market some necklaces she'd designed, plus I tutored children in hospitals who were too sick to go to school. Then a girlfriend who'd worked at the Chanel cosmetic counter at Filene's, who'd become the manager of the Nars counter at Saks, offered me a freelance make-up artist job. We did so much volume that I started working for Nars six days a week. Before I knew it, I was working seven days a week, for Christian Dior, Bobby Brown, Laura Mercier, and Yves Saint Laurent as well.

My watershed moment was realizing, I'm working at a department store seven days a week just to make maybe $700? With my degree? I started making a list of things I knew how to do well. Each thing by itself was not convincing; I was like, 'I'm a good dinner party hostess? Oh, great—that won't get me a bus pass!' I was starting to get a little disheartened. But when I looked at the list as a whole, I was looking for a skill set I could market, and I thought, putting these skills together, I think I have something here!

"I thought, you know, there are a lot of people who just don't have finesse. This country could use an expert who'd teach people to have finesse! That was the moment my company Polished Information was born. It was a light bulb moment. Within a week or two, I had ordered business cards, written up a brochure, designed a logo, sent word to all of the local magazines and TV shows in Boston, got a four-page spread in *The Improper Bostonian* newspaper, and a four-minute segment on the Fox affiliate! One thing fed the next, and I started to get clients.

"My mom was a fashion designer; she was one of these early-seventies career women, so I used to go to her studio as a kid and play with fabric swatches. I knew what chartreuse was before I could spell my name! My mother was a HUGE, enormous influence—everything from soup to nuts had to look a certain way with my mother, and everything was about appearances. That was a great training ground. Plus, I had a friend who owned a pattern service in the garment district for a lot of the couture houses. I would manage his office and work as a fit model for some of his clients. These past details figured into the business. With my dance and movement skills, I could teach clients how to walk better, have better posture. I help clients with personal appearance based on my make-up skills. Having taken directing classes helps me see the big picture and put it all together for my clients.

"I do more than dress people; I redo their social calendars. I help them find mates. I help them with job interviews. I help people take control of their destinies, as I took control of mine, and package themselves better so that they get what they want.

"I've learned this: never rationalize. Be honest with yourself; know who you are, and who you're not. Don't take no for an answer, and dream big. Dream REALLY big! You just have to have enough guts to try to do the impossible."

nine
closing the deal

Selling yourself is one of the acting profession's ten command-ments. Some performers don't like the marketing aspect of their careers so much. To them getting new headshots and updating the old resume with that Pop Tarts commercial that only ran after 3:00 AM in Alaska is a major intrusion on pursuing their craft. You can't get in to wow the casting director with your method power, though, if you don't take care of the necessary promotional details.

Some actors actually love the salesmanship that entertainment work demands, though. Many love it so much, they incorporate it into their lives as an entirely new career. What follows are the stories of three very empowered actor/businesspeople who've found they've truly come into their own through mastering the art of the deal.

TOP OF THE FOOD CHAIN

It's around 6:30 AM and Cooper Bates is getting out of bed in his Los Angeles home. He sits down at his desk immediately and writes a romantic e-mail to his wife, who's at Bates's second home in

Oaxaca with their two young children. Then he goes to get some hot tea, and writes out material for various work projects for the next three hours.

At nearly 10:00 AM, Bates arrives at his office, and starts plowing through e-mail and rolling out phone calls. He's then off to a meeting every day—either production, marketing, or sales, which lasts about two hours. Working at his desk through the afternoon, he sips only lemon water and stevia, which doesn't bog him down and make him as sleepy as a heavy lunch.

Now it's 7:00 PM, and Bates is finally ready to eat. He leaves the office to go get a salad and on the way to pick it up, makes another phone call or two. Then it's back to the office for even more work. Evenings are when he can do heavy proposal writing without interruption; he usually wraps things up around ten. He heads home, chats for a while with his roommate, who is also a co-worker, and goes to bed around 2:00 AM, to do it all again barely five hours later.

Is Bates a software whiz? An accountant? A Hollywood agent? No—he's an actor turned co-founder and CEO of a multimillion-dollar company. Hint Mint, the product Bates and his partner, former child star Harley Cross, started in April 2000, has exploded beyond the duo's wildest expectations. This delicious, healthy little breath freshener is vegan, containing no gelatin, aspartame, or animal ingredients, and comes in a curvy, stylish tin (the tins themselves have become extremely hot collectibles on the Internet). Hint Mint's initial retail order was for a modest 750 units; ten months later, ten million units were sold. In the United States and England, its exclusive markets span W Hotels, Harvey Nichols, and Harrods department stores.

How the heck did all of this happen? First, Bates offers a little history. "After I graduated from college, I followed a girl to Waco, Texas. We broke up, and I decided I'd go to California to pursue acting," he recalls. "I was telling a woman I knew my aspirations, and she said, 'I wouldn't go to California—I'd go to Texas because it's a right-to-work state.' There'd be more opportunity. So I took off for Dallas, and did the whole starving-artist thing—slept in my car for the first few days, and cleaned up in McDonald's bathrooms. I ended up joining an acting studio, which I thought made sense because I could sneak in at night and sleep in the school. It also seemed really attractive, because I'd be acting all day long. That was very cool."

Success came quickly. "I got my first job, I can't really remember, a commercial or something," he continues. "At the time, there were only five major casting directors in Dallas, and it took some work, but once you got in to see them, but once you were in, you were in. You could make a name for yourself, because the market wasn't very big. I started doing all of this theater, and then a casting director called me and said, 'Hey, would you be interested in being an extra on *Robocop*?' I said, 'God, no.' She said, 'Cooper, you do this for me! They really want a good actor!' So I did it, it was first time on a real set, and they kept stretching out my part, and moving me around from scene to scene. Everybody really embraced me in Dallas; I'd be introduced to someone, and they'd be told, 'Joe, Cooper's an actor,' and Joe would roll his eyes. But then he'd be told, 'Cooper's a REAL actor—he works!' "

In 1987, Bates found himself cast in a movie called *Cohen & Tate*, with Roy Scheider and Adam Baldwin. Harley Cross was the child actor in it, and that's where the two future moguls met. "He was nine, I was twenty-one. Harley was really influential, because he's already done all these leads in all these films, at nine years old. We kept in touch."

Soon after, Bates saw his career go through some changes. "The beginning of my degeneration as an actor, I guess, was that people started coddling me too much," he says. "I had a lot of moderate success in Dallas, and these acting teachers would come out from Los Angeles and tell me, 'Wow, you're amazing, you're really talented!' It sped up my desire to go out to LA, but I wasn't prepared. The difference between a Los Angeles resume and a Dallas resume are night and day. I went out, auditioned for *Designing Women*, didn't get it, but met a casting director who put me up for *Days of Our Lives*. I worked on that as a day player twice a month for two years. I also did a soap called *Generations*. I also did lots of showcases—there was this place where you could go and pay twenty-five bucks to see a casting director. I met my agent that way, got a couple commercials that way. So that was pretty much my acting career."

Meanwhile, he and Cross had been keeping in touch. "He would come out to LA from New York for pilot season and sleep on my couch," remembers Bates. "It wasn't like we'd ever talked about starting a business together, because we were wedded to acting, obviously. But his career started slowing down a little bit, too—he went from doing a couple of films and a series a year to one film a year. He was also growing up, starting to travel, picking up other interests. When Harley was around seventeen, he told me he had an idea for a breath mint called Hint Mint. The joke was, it was a hint (you needed one) and he thought he could sell it. I said, 'Great.' I was really into this self-made model where I wasn't going to discourage anybody, because you never knew if magic could happen. So I didn't know how to encourage him, but didn't want to discourage him, either. He'd talk about this idea all the time, and then about two years later, he asked me, 'Would you help me produce this?' I was shooting short films at the time, trying to forge my way into directing. Harley thought producing the product must be like producing a film, finding all the sources and putting things together. I said, 'I'd be happy to.'"

Within a few weeks Bates had found manufacturers for both mints and mint tins. "Harley had gotten us an attorney, and made a business card. We made a prototype, and it came out beautifully!" Thrown into the fire, they suddenly had product deadlines to meet: "It went from us working four hours a day to working eighteen hours a day almost overnight."

Bates found the business surprisingly adaptable for an artist. "A lot of the elements of this particular company had the same elements acting, writing, or directing have for me, meaning the more creative you could be, the more people would be drawn to what you were doing," he explains. "After we got our first sale of two hundred fifty mint tins to Bristol Farms (a popular store in the Los Angeles area) Harley told me how much money we could potentially make. At the time, I was really poor; I was subsisting on maybe six or seven thousand dollars a year. I had also fallen in love with traveling, so my initial argument was that I wasn't interested in making money, in trading my time, that I enjoyed traveling and my own company too much. But Harley kept harping on it, and as he was talking to me, I looked over wherever we were and saw somebody pull a tube of Chap Stick and they used it, and the person next to that person asked, 'Do you mind if I use it?' And I just thought that was so beautiful, that there's a product that somebody saw in a store, bought it, and was sharing it now. I thought, wherever I go in the world, I could see this product, and I helped develop it. So I committed myself fully."

It paid off; the company became a roaring success. For Bates, his only concern was time away from his wife and kids. "My family moved to Oaxaca to educate our five- and seven-year-olds in Spanish," he says. "I came back, though, had a talk with the boys here, and we said, 'If we give this thing one more committed year, we'll take it to another level, and then we'll all reassess. So I decided to do that, but at the sacrifice of my family, who are still living in Oaxaca. I didn't want my children to lose out on the experience they're having. So I go back and forth. We have a pretty nice place down there."

When Bates is by himself in LA, he definitely makes the most of things. "I've nourished my creativity and curiosity," he states. "The pursuits I became invested in have made me a relatively interesting person to myself. When I'm by myself, I like my company." There's lots more work to keep him even busier as well; Hint Mint is now going gangbusters in the international market, selling in over fifteen countries, and is a huge pop culture craze in Japan.

For Bates, one of the greatest gifts the success of Hint Mint has brought is peace of mind. "I remember once looking out our bay window onto the landscape, and there's nothing but trees and rolling hills, and it's just gorgeous," he says. "I thought, man, I have a house here, I have a house in Los Angeles, can travel a lot, love my amazing family—and I suddenly got nervous. Then I thought, wait a sec, I don't have to be nervous about anything. It's not like I ever have to start all over and try to get here again. That really gave me a lot of comfort."

RAZZLE-DAZZLE 'EM

Brian Keith Lewis is truly a shooting star in the high pressure, high profit world of real estate. A veteran performer with credits encompassing film, TV, Off Broadway, and numerous Broadway workshops, Lewis has pursued his entertainment goals with a fiery ambition. When he elected to take on the Manhattan housing market as well, he shrewdly made his mark with a combination of life experience, big confidence, and high energy. Here's his story:

"We moved a lot when I was a kid, and that plays into both acting and real estate for me. My dad was a sales guy who didn't rest on his laurels—he was always moving on to the next thing, self-taught, Man of the Year with the Sara Lee Corporation. Anytime he would get a promotion, we would up and go. Going into new, fresh situations like that, you get to decide who you want to be the next year.

You take the attributes of the people you liked at your last school and wear them, kind of like a role.

"I'm extroverted; I love people, get my energy from others. Given that, in each new school, I'd audition for plays, because my brother Greg was the fine athlete, and I was just a good athlete. I wanted to do something I excelled at, something he did not do. I had a one-man show my senior year in high school at Busch Gardens in Virginia. It was a terrific twenty-minute show; I did it five times a day. Then I went on to William & Mary, where I got a very large head, because I got a lot of things I wanted there. After one year, I decided, 'I need conservatory training, because I'm a SERIOUS ACT-AH.' So I left for the School of the Arts in North Carolina. I intended to spend four years, but only spent a semester, because I discovered most of my peers were using it as a graduate school, they were much older than me, and frankly, I needed more stimulation mentally. It was amazing voice training, body training, etc., but that's all we did, morning noon and night—theater.

I went back to William & Mary, finished my studies, and moved to Manhattan. I couch-surfed with the best of them, and auditioned. I got into Uta Hagen's class, and was able to study with Uta for a couple of years before she started working again. I was so excited, because you have to audition and be asked to join. While I was doing that, I got a manager who got me involved with commercials, so I got to sink my teeth into those and voice-overs. The voice-over world is a very small niche, and I've never stopped doing them—to this day, I book, I do, and I love 'em.

"Movie-wise, I did *A Beautiful Mind*; I was Russell Crowe's stand-in. I'd never, ever done that work, and I don't want to do it again. I actually had to audition for Russell. I had to meet with him, sit with him, and also talk and meet with Roger Deakins, the director of photography. Very famous people. The thing about it is, you're not a member of the crew—they don't really claim you—and you're not really an actor in it, but you have to be unobtrusively present all the time. But I thought, why not spend three and a half, four months on an A-list film set, with the likes of Ron Howard and Russell Crowe, standing with them, listening to them, watching them, every single shot of this movie? There's my film school, and I got paid for it. And Ron arranged it so I got a nice day player credit in the movie, so I get residuals on that.

"This was all while doing real estate, mind you. I'd been doing a Broadway workshop with two stars from *Miss Saigon*, and I heard one ask the other, 'Hey, are you going to that closing tomorrow?' 'No, will you do it for me?' 'OK!' They were in real estate, too. They told me, 'We're good at it, but you would be GREAT at it!' Then we had an actors' strike. I was hoofing bags at a hotel, and I thought, wow, I'm thirty years old, I've got two degrees, and I'm carrying bags. Not that there's anything wrong with that. But I found out about the Actors' Work Program, went in, answered a bunch of questions, and was asked, 'Have you ever considered real estate?' I was like, 'OK! How do I do it?' I found a school, took my class, met another actor who did real estate and told me, 'You should meet my management at Halstead [a real estate company].' I met at Halstead, and started working at Halstead.

"At Halstead, you're an independent contractor; you only get paid for your closings. You can spend one hour and make a million dollars, or spend a million hours and make one dollar. It's not the magic wand a lot of actors think—it's about self-motivation, big-time. Now, I have flexibility in my schedule. I schedule auditions and bookings as if they are showings at an apartment.

"I think because actors are always waiting for permission to work, we're almost like whipped puppies. If you want to be a star, you don't have to be an actor, just be Paris Hilton. If you want to be a working actor, find out what your skills are, and just exploit them. Create an environment where you can use them. Don't wait for the mail to come. Create your own buzz, always be honest, and the world will respond to your truth.

"I feel that so much of my fellow 'carny trash'—that's what I affectionately call the artists that I love, and I'm one of them—have a bit of arrested development. We hang on to this idea of suffering for our art. We don't know what it's like to go away for a long weekend, or have a nice apartment. You wake up, you're fifty-five, and you're hanging out in the Equity lounge—somehow, there's a disconnect. You're playing people who are in the world, but you're so disconnected from the world as an 'artist,' you can't interpret it anymore. So get in there and hang out with all types of people!

"I'm motivated by excellence. I'm not motivated by money. It just happens to be that things that I do are attractive to people, and they give me money for them. I don't like to need. Neediness for me creates an environment where I can't be creative. Not needing for me creates an environment where I feel safe, and I feel creative. Doing real estate provides me with a certain level of not-needing. I don't go in there thinking, 'I have to have this, because I need to eat!' For me, I don't thrive from that place. I need to feel fulfilled, happy, safe, and loved. If when I was training, there was a teacher who didn't make me feel any of those things, I'd fire 'em. I create a world where those things are always around me.

"Real estate has worked very well for me because it's liberated me. It calls upon skills I have—people skills, organizational skills, communication skills. Every actor shouldn't jump into real estate; I've seen many actors flounder and falter. Time is money in real estate, and nobody's gonna wait for you to dance. People like attractive energy around them. If you feel attractive while teaching kindergarten or working in a wood shop, than do what makes YOU feel good.

"I loved seeing my name in the *New York Times*. I loved when newer brokers come to ask me for advice. I loved when the company made in me a senior vice president in only five years. I loved when I'm named top producer for a certain quarter, or top producer in the entire West Side office, because we have a hell of a lot good brokers. Those aren't goals, they just happen because you keep doing good stuff. I have so much more to learn in this life, so much more to learn about acting, so many more goals in real estate. I like the closings—they're a kick. I'm selling an apartment at the Hampshire House for nearly $5 million! In theater, all you ever want is the opening, and in real estate, all I ever want is the closing!

"I try not to give my day to anybody till I've had my day, meaning, I've gotta get up, eat well, and work out. I might have two or three auditions. I'm incessant about e-mail and voicemails, because in my business, communication is the key. You run downtown for a voice-over, you have an (apartment) showing, you're creating a show sheet for a new exclusive, you're meeting a seller, you work through lunch. To me, this isn't a nine-to-five thing, it's a lifestyle; it's not like, 'At 5:00, I'm no longer a broker.' I've done walk-throughs at 10:30 at night. And then some days, you don't have much.

"I'm known for my work for sellers. In this market, that's a strength. Markets can change on a dime, and if they do, trust me, I'll be the best buyers' broker out there. But at this point, I love sellers because I love creating a production—getting the property, scoring the exclusive, and shepherding that into the marketplace. Open house days are opening night! You're playing yourself—although some actors don't like that. I like playing myself!

"Success means that my skill set and the things I value are being nurtured, encouraged, and developed. When those things are happening, and all engines are running, the universe will just say 'yes.' When all of my natural skills and abilities are being rewarded, I'm getting yeses because of me."

THE GIRL WITH SOMETHING EXTRA

Ayo Haynes has always been a super-achiever. An excellent student, she went after her educational goals with laser-like focus. The acting career she's always dreamt of suddenly became a reality, and she's made the most of every opportunity that's come her way.

Now, she's a major player in the business world: as an event organizer for 8 Minute Dating, the nationwide industry leader in speed dating singles parties. Here, Haynes discusses her past, present and future accomplishments and goals; her story offers some sage life lessons any smart person should draw from.

Lesson One: Know Your Strengths

"Acting started in a weird way. All throughout high school, I wanted to be an actress but I didn't have the nerve or guts to admit that. I went to a really advanced high school, where you're supposed to become a doctor, lawyer, scientist, something very professional. To say that you wanted to be an actor was frowned upon.

"I kind of pushed it out of my head. I ended up going to a five-year BA/MBA business school program at Bentley College outside Boston. I was going to become a whiz kid down on Wall Street. It wasn't until my junior year that I was doing some work at a temp agency for the summer, and as luck would have it, they put me at a dance/theater production company, answering phones. Complete serendipity! One of the guys there reading scripts for the owner was at Columbia for playwrighting, and he was doing his thesis, and I talked my way into his play, basically. I could talk my way into anything.

"The director, Michael Henry Brown, was being touted as the next great thing in the theater world. He then asked me to be in a staged reading, and then that same summer, I was onstage with

Delroy Lindo and all of these great Broadway stars. I was like, this is what I want to do! I'm like, nineteen, twenty at this point."

Lesson Two: Strike While the Iron Is Hot

"I basically had to bide my time till I graduated. Carla Brothers, an actress who'd been in the staged reading, introduced me to her agents over at Abrams, and they basically let me know that being in Boston and trying to come to the city for auditions just wasn't feasible, but if I was really serious, in the summertime, they'd be happy to send me out. I told my mother I didn't want to pursue my MBA anymore, and she told me, 'You've lost your mind. You're finishing your degree!' So I finished the degree on time.

"Within my first week back in New York, I'd booked a kids' show called *Way Cool*. I was a replacement for Lisa Gay Hamilton, and it was such great training. A few years later, I did *Another World*; I got cast to play, basically, Mary, delivering the baby on Christmas Eve. The casting director for that soap, Jimmy Bore, called me later out of the blue asking if I was available to work on *As The World Turns*. I didn't have to audition; when I saw the script, it was a major part, and I was like, 'Oh, my God!'

Lesson Three: Think Fast When You Need To

"You get used to the money on a soap opera. I had been blessed throughout my career that I only had to do some temp work during my first couple of years. I had done commercials, but wasn't really booking them while I was on the soap. When my job on the soap ended, I was having a serious cash flow problem. I was like, what could I do, and what could I enjoy doing?

"I've always had a knack for meeting people, for being able to network and put the right people together. I've always liked match-making. So I'd played around with the idea of having parties where I'd have my friends bring their single friends, but really didn't know how to go about it. I knew to be successful at it would take computer infrastructure I didn't want to put the time and money into. So one day I just happened to have *The John Walsh Show* on TV, and it was about dating companies. I wrote down every single one of the companies on the show. I took into account what I liked and disliked about each person presenting his or her company. Then I did a lot of research on the Internet, and found that 8 Minute Dating had the most proliferation, basically. So I applied.

"We had set up this meeting, and I hadn't gotten a confirmation the day of, so being the go-getter that I am, I just stopped by their offices. They were like, no one ever does that. You really have to have confidence and a plan of action. I knew I wanted to go to the Bronx High School of Science in the third grade, so I started taking prep tests in fifth grade! Anyway, during my interview at 8 Minute Dating, I asked THEM questions. I was interviewing them as much as they were interviewing me. How do I get paid? How do I know you're gonna pay me on time? If I'm gonna put this effort forward to sell 8 Minute Dating under your umbrella, then I need to know you're a company I want to be affiliated with.

"I came on board to do what I thought was a hole in the market, African-American dating events. I didn't want to be known as ONLY the event organizer for African-Americans, however; I also knew I could pull people from a wide variety of circles. I did many events for many age groups. Doing event organizing gave me the opportunity to still keep my days free, and not be exhausted for auditions and acting jobs."

Lesson Four: Know What's Best for You

"I am good at a lot of things, and that's a blessing and a curse. You could get easily sidetracked by the thing you're good at that you don't mind doing, but where does that leave you in the end? Event organizing is a constant reminder of, yes, I'm good at this, but it's not what I set up a production company for! Yes, I produce events on a large scale, and I've increased my negotiation skills networking that way, but it's about, OK, I need time to accomplish goals acting-wise and career-wise.

"My father passed away on the night I had an event. I was going to have a woman from a cable network profile me. Being the professional you're supposed to be, the show must go on, and talking to her, I was telling her I'd meet her at the event and breaking down in tears. This woman said, 'Ayo, what are you doing? Cancel this event!' I was like, 'No, all these people are counting on me!' She said, 'Forget it!' It slowed me down, and made me think about what is REALLY important, and I took a time out over the summer to do just that. I had been doing four events a week; you're constantly monitoring the number of people attending, making sure your numbers are even, making sure the venues are set up, preparing your paperwork. So I only did one event over the summer, and did my most prosperous event, Professional Singles 25–35, which took no extra energy or effort on my part."

Lesson Five: Do It 100 Percent

"I pride myself on my events. From the beginning, I thought, why would I want to attend one of my own events? I would want to attend if I was going to get something for free, or win something. So I went to different spots around the Chelsea area and said to the business owners, 'Hey, I've got fifty single professionals with lots of disposable income who need to know about your business. If you give away a great prize to my attendees, I'll give you free space on the Web site to hyperlink to your site, and be taken to any page on your Web site to market to them.' I was able to do that with several companies and keep them as partners a year and a half later—New York Sports Clubs, *Sweet Charity*, some Off Broadway shows, and restaurant associations. To me, it was always about, 'What do I need to make my job of filling up the event easier? I need to get things associated with my event that nobody else has, so that people will be immediately attracted to my event and sign up on their own.' I think that's one way I distinguish myself from other event organizers."

Lesson Six: Keep Your Eyes on the Prize

"I always realized there was a niche in the market for speed-networking businesses and organizations. I've been doing that with cosmetic executive women, *Fortune Magazine*. Now, again, I'm transitioning out of working with someone else, as an independent contractor, with a middleman getting some of my money, to specifically targeting a niche market. It's been exploding.

"On a daily basis, I'm also auditioning for commercials and voice-overs, plus corporate diversity training. I'm helping a friend cast a project. I don't know how I find all the hours in the day to do all this! I'm still waiting to see which direction everything will take me in. I've kind of learned to let go of the steering wheel, so to speak. I still have my hands on the wheel, but I'm not trying to direct the car, I'm going with the flow and seeing where everything takes me. I know that each of the areas in the acting and entertainment fields I'm working in are undeniably leading me back to a special dream I had in college, to combine my business and artistic talents within my own production company, where I will produce my own projects. I want to sell a documentary, and some lifestyle programming shows.

"My measure of success is still developing. I have so much more to achieve, so much more that I want to accomplish!"

ten
twenty-four-hour party people

Actors are essentially people-pleasers—a powerful asset for becoming successful in the entertainment industry. Some are simply born with the knack to entertain and love wowing an audience on a solely artistic level. Some seek approval and self-worth through a crowd's applause. And some simply love give-and-take on a human, altruistic level—for these actors, it's all about taking pride in making other people happy.

The artist-businesspeople profiled in this chapter all definitely fall into that last category. Highly successful on their own terms as creative forces, they've also made their marks through providing those services that make the world go round—music, food, drink. They all share a ferocious work ethic, plus savvy minds when it comes to combining making a living with making their art. Read on as they discuss the fruits of true labor.

FEEL GOOD, INC.

It's early morning, and even though he doesn't have to work until tonight, DJ Darryl Palmer is already preparing for his job. He busies himself gathering up a plethora of electronic equipment and CDs. Then he starts poring over his meticulously organized music planner, thinking about what song's going to go where during the wedding he'll be working at—"especially in the early hours of the event, because that's when you get people's attention, get them having fun, get them relaxed," he explains. "Once you've achieved that, things roll easily all evening long."

Palmer's business, The Singing DJ, has made him one of Canada's most in-demand live event entertainers. He runs the operation with his wife and managing partner, Arlene, a former ad copywriter from the United States. Fueled by a combination of Darryl's previous experience as a successful stage, film, and TV actor and Arlene's sterling business mind, bookings are off the charts. The Palmers next intend to make inroads into the US market; Darryl has already played a smash-hit gig in Las Vegas.

"I had lots of positive feedback as a singer as a kid, and it stayed with me forever," Darryl recalls. "In school, I started doing some acting, and that led to musicals at the University of Western Ontario in London, Ontario. I later did roles like Freddy in *My Fair Lady*."

He started working in radio. "I got my early experience on the CBC in Montreal, doing research and musical work," he continues. "There is quite a fine film industry in Toronto, so as soon as I moved here, I became a member of the acting union, doing films and commercials.

"In between Darryl's acting jobs, he was singing with two different live bands, then started his own band," Arlene adds. "He got very fed up and frustrated, because it was difficult keeping the band together. They were performing at private parties, cocktail parties, and weddings. He said one day he wished he could control the music all the time. Going to many social events, he noticed that someone was always turning up the volume to a distorted level, and Darryl would sort of take over, and the music would be great. People would compliment him. He saw an opportunity to take a certified course to be a disk jockey, and decided that would be a great way to combine his musical knowledge and his ability to create a great sound in a room (a very unique talent) and a way to control all the music, all the time. Plus, he'd be able to sing; he could then use music minus one-type playback, and develop a repertoire to do a live performance while he deejays, with a great CD backup. I said, hey, we'll be able to offer the best of both worlds: live excitement, plus ten thousand songs, while a band is really limited. We could really tailor events to what a client wants, plus sound quality and musical quality could be controlled."

Darryl took the course, and then Arlene got to work on advertising. "The one thing performers aren't good at is selling themselves— it's very difficult," she explains. "Given my marketing and advertising background, I decided I would jump in and help that end of the business, to get clients. Darryl also has a degree in computer science, so we came across a list of two hundred corporations. I took this massive list, and smiled and dialed. I called every single one of them. Some friends in the business generously made up a little promotion for us, to get Christmas bookings in the summer. I called these companies, to kind of get to the decision-making people, and ask if we could send this information. We did—we did a mailing, and I followed up, and we started to get them."

People were curious about what the Singing DJ did, exactly, at first. "When Darryl starts to sing at an event, people's jaws drop, and there's a big swell of excitement," Arlene reports. "The testimonials we get back from our clients are embarrassingly positive."

By now it's early afternoon, and Darryl's packed up his car with the equipment and his wardrobe. He does his vocal warm-up while driving about an hour to tonight's job location, arriving at the event hall by mid-afternoon. "Most of my events are six or seven hours long, from six PM to one AM, so I'm arriving two or three hours before the music is required," he explains. He moves things in, sets up his stage, figures out where the lights and speakers are going to go and how things will play in the room.

It's just about six PM now. "As people start to arrive, I've always got some groovy, energizing music going," Darryl enthuses. "This usually works well—people start tapping their toes or jumping around a bit the minute they notice it, and feel good. That's what I'm looking for."

After some intro tunes, Darryl grabs the mike and sings a few numbers during cocktails. This is typical for his performance, but uncommon for most event entertainers to attempt. "My warm-up has given me lots of juice and confidence, so I'm ready to cruise right into some great vocals at the first opportunity," Darryl explains. "This seems to intrigue and amuse people, and they'll sometimes even get on the dance floor during cocktail hour; that gives me a thrill, because that's a very good sign that they're ready to party and have a good time."

He continues the festive vibe during dinner, performing some swing tunes. Then after the meal, it's time to really crank out the showstoppers. "After dinner, I always have a great number ready, something I know is going to appeal to the crowd, maybe that has to do with the age of the crowd, or the theme of the company," he confides. " 'Lady in Red' fills the dance floor with all age groups; so does a Bobby Darin or Sinatra tune. But if you want to talk about big winners, a disco tune like 'That's the Way I Like It' will always get people going!"

Five hours later, Daryl is still singing and mixing tunes, "because people may go out for a drink or smoke or something, but once they come back, they'll boogie down for another half hour or so," he comments. "I did a party of thirty people the other night who danced straight from 9:30 to 1 o'clock." The meticulous prep he puts into choosing songs pays off. "Probably one of the most demanding parts of the work is mixing the tunes just right, so there's not too much fast stuff, or too much slow stuff," he elaborates. "I meet [with clients] and question them as to what kind of music they like—my planner contains about twenty different types of music, with artists listed under each style. I hear, 'We love this!', or 'I never want to hear that!', that sort of thing. So armed with that information, I have a playlist in mind."

It's finally the end of the night. Darryl turns off his lights, and packs up within the hour. Any last tricks of the trade he wants to mention? "I always leave 'em begging for one or two more songs," he says good-naturedly. And then he starts his car and heads for home, so he can do it all again tomorrow night.

BACK HOME AGAIN

With her electric blue hair extensions and sunny personality, Tammy Tanner has infused fresh energy into her hometown of Granby, Connecticut. After sixteen years performing a high-energy cabaret act across the globe, Tanner returned to her old stomping grounds to open June's Diner, an old-school eatery named to honor her late mother. A smart businesswoman as well as a pioneering artist, Tanner tells how she's navigated both adventurous paths in her life.

"Everybody always knew I'd get into music. My whole family was musical. My parents were both professional musicians in the 1940s; my father was a saxophone player who played with Stan Kenton, and my mother sang, and that's how they met.

"Growing up, I sang with the church choir, and sang solos, and I was pretty relaxed with people staring at me. There was a little piano in my brother's room, and I'd sneak in there and play some chords. Then I started getting good, so through my dad's local musical contacts, a man named Ray Caserino became my piano teacher—an incredible jazz player and teacher, just incredible. I was influenced by Stevie Wonder, Liza Minnelli, the Manhattan Transfer, the Beatles, and David Cassidy! I'm never growing up—I still go to David Cassidy concerts today! He's actually a really good, serious performer!

"I went on to the Berklee College of Music. Berklee is amazing now, but it really wasn't quite as amazing when I was there. I was really disillusioned because a lot of people were using drugs, and I'm totally not into that at all. People also sounded kind of the same— there was this kind of jazz solo-crazy thing going on. That's not what I wanted; I wanted to just play normal songs that normal people could understand and sing along with.

"I just wanted to perform, and learn to perform. I figured out, the real way to perform is to throw yourself into the lion's den, and sink or swim. I got a job as a musical director for a singer with an amazing voice, Kathy Marquette—she's like a cross between Billie Holiday and Mama Cass. We did a cabaret thing, which gave me lots of experience in stage banter.

"Then I went on tour with a musical comedy about eating disorders called *Food Fight*. We played colleges all over the east coast, and the woman who wrote the music for the show had played in Sweden. She gave my phone number to an agent in Atlanta who works with a huge circuit of piano bars in Scandinavia. At the same time, my mother was very sick, and ended up passing away, the biggest nightmare you can imagine. Literally a few days before her funeral, the agent had me on the phone going over the last details for the audition—I didn't tell anybody what was going on in my life, they wouldn't have hired me, I'm sure. But I got the job. I was supposed to be gone three months, and the first year I was gone ten and a half months. My mother died in September, and I went overseas in January—I had planned to go to Key West and cry my eyes out for a whole bunch of months. It was like someone had picked me up and cradled me and took care of me, though, through those first months without her.

"Scandinavia is not exactly the most bright and fluffy place in the middle of winter. I learned how to say one thing in Swedish: 'I would like to learn to speak Swedish.' So nobody spoke English to me for a month, then I was finally able to talk! After working in the south of Sweden, I popped over to Copenhagen, and played at this big carnival over there, and there were all of these tulips everywhere. It was the first time I really saw color in a year. I said, 'OK, I think this is all going to be all right.'

"One thing led to another: I did nice piano bars in nice hotels. I went to Norway, and looking for fun one night, walked into this huge piano club called Zakken. I was like, wow, I wanna do this! There was a male pianist from Kansas playing there at the time, and I met the owners and asked if they'd ever had a girl play. They said, 'We've tried, but nobody's really strong enough to do it.' I said, 'I would love to try.' I did a fifteen-minute audition, and they told me they wanted me as soon as possible.

"Zakken was like a cross between a piano bar and a discotheque; I've never seen anything like it in the US. The house size was 1,500, and there were huge video screens everywhere, on two levels. I was amazed, because the audience knew all of the words to every one of my songs in English! I was the only woman on the circuit, and had my own style of playing Paul Simon and Aretha Franklin. I was moving it—I did a Tina Turner thing in a wig, jumped up on the piano! I started getting critique from my colleagues that I was changing the concept of the whole piano bar thing—it was really becoming a show. But I was all about giving the people what they wanted, when they wanted it. Eventually, though, there were changes in management, communication problems, so I moved on. I started working most of the time at a club called Frakken, the greatest club of this kind in the world. It's a great organization that gets great people to come in and do their thing. I worked with them, and with their entertainment management, and it was a fabulous experience both artistically and business-wise.

"Still, I'd known for a while it was going to be time to do something else—after all, how many times can I sing 'It's Raining

Men'? I had developed my niche and my image and it worked, it was just a drag to get on a plane and fly across the world, especially after September 11. I also didn't want to find myself at eighty years old, sitting there playing 'Hotel California.' I figured I'd buy a restaurant or nightclub or something in Hartford, Connecticut, never in my hometown of Granby, because I like my privacy. My family owns a small airport in Massachusetts, which we inherited from my father in 1998. I figured I'd add some food service and entertainment there, as we wanted to sell it, and it would increase the value. But it's difficult to organize a family dynamic as a business dynamic.

"My brother Glenn is very high up in the restaurant hierarchy—he runs the fine dining restaurant Raffles in Singapore. He had read this article in the *New York Times* online about people buying old diners and re-opening them. For about thirty seconds, we thought we'd buy an old diner and put it at the airport, except we're really good friends, so why would we want to own a restaurant together? I was sick of traveling all over the world, but this diner thing was perfect for what I'd always envisioned. What I'd wanted to own was exactly what a diner is—a friendly place with good, homemade food, and I would try to add live entertainment. I asked Glenn, 'Do you mind if I steal the idea and run with it?' and he said, 'Go ahead.'

"It made more sense for me to do it in my own town, because I'd built the perfect house—my house is a cluster of three domes connected to one another—I have the most perfect dog, so why do I want to work an hour and a half away? I started looking into property in my town, found what I like. I'm doing a land lease from a totally fun lawyer who owns it, a really nice guy.

"Everybody really gets it. In my town, we have eight pizza places and another just opened—it's just too stupid in a town of 11,000 people. When I first came with the idea, and sent it to the town planner, who sent it to the planning and zoning commission for an informal comment, everybody was like, 'Wow! It sounds interesting! And it's not a pizza house!' Everybody knows me; everybody knew my father, because he owned the gas station in town. All of a sudden, I'm coming back to do something that's not just a product we clearly need, it's really good for the community.

"The diner itself is really historic. It's a sixty-five-year-old piece of incredible engineering. I've studied hundreds and hundreds of menus. I've named the diner after my mother, so I want the food to be in the style she'd expect from me. Some family recipes, but it's all about good, old-fashioned comfort food, served with style—and live music, of course!"

LEGEND IN HER OWN TIME

Kelly Ford Wohlford has established herself in a variety of professional areas—as a longtime New York actress, a recording engineer/producer/singer/songwriter at the legendary Massachusetts recording studio Longview Farm, as a teacher of the arts to young children. Wohlford also gets a serious kick out of her work as a singing, acting, and dancing waitress at the Medieval Manor in Boston. This well-known theater-restaurant is packed nightly with oafs, jesters, royalty, wenches, and patrons being force-fed bowls of dragon soup (while loving every minute of it). Wohlford clues us in on the secrets to working in such a wild and crazy establishment, and talks about her many major career accomplishments.

Back to Her Roots

"I went to a small college in Davenport, Iowa. A lot of the people there were looking to get teaching degrees, but I was interested in performing. I ended up taking off a year to put some money in the bank, working at a dinner theater called Circa 21. I met a lot of people from New York, Chicago, different theater communities around the country. I moved to New York after that year; I had always pictured myself in New York, on Broadway.

"I got a couple of waitressing jobs, and did some cabaret in the piano bars down in the Village. It's very hard to get to the upper level of music and theater in New York. The first few years I was in New York, I auditioned a lot. You can either audition, audition, audition, hoping for your Equity Card, waiting to be a star—or you can work all the time. I really wanted to work. I never turned down work of any kind. I always worked non-union. You have to work a lot harder, and you have to manage your money better, but there's a lot of good theater and good music getting produced, new musicals, short original plays. You didn't really make any money doing those, but you got in on the ground floor, originating roles, being part of the development process. That's interesting! I always enjoyed creating characters, and that kind of thing was at arm's reach for me all the time."

Time to Change

"The transition for me started when I fried my voice. I was hired to sing at the comedy club Catch a Rising Star, and I did some demo singing, and I was very tired. My vocal cords were inflamed, so I had to stop singing for a month. I went to the doctor, started taking steroids, was talking to another friend who'd had nodes a few years earlier, and she told me about a teacher who did holistic singing; she'd worked with Rod Stewart and Annie Lennox. I went to her and auditioned to study, got picked. I met a lot of people through her, started writing and collaborating with people. I started getting hired to sing back-up on records, and the more time I spent in the studio, the more I loved audio. I took a course in audio engineering. There aren't a lot of women who do this, but I did very well, and got offered an internship at the Longview Farm. I'm still there today, on staff now; Longview's my second home!"

Hearing Her Calling Again

"At Longview, I started engineering, producing, singing back-up. There was so much for me to do. I started a children's choir, and wrote lots of songs. But I really wasn't done with theater. I had the itch to give it one more try. At that point, I hadn't been in a theatrical production for years. I decided to audition for a community theater show, to get my feet wet again. I did a terrific audition for *Jesus Christ Superstar*; it was between me and another woman who'd been with this particular company for a really long time, and they ended up going with her for that reason. I was offered a spot in the chorus, but it wasn't what I was looking for, so I declined. Then I got a call from the woman who did get cast in the role. She was working at the Medieval Manor, too, and said, 'Would you be interested in working there? You've got a terrific voice, and they really need women.' I hadn't heard of it before, so she invited me to see the show, and then I could decide. So I went."

Middle Ages Madness

"The show was goofy, bawdy, sick jokes, a lot of fun! The thing that impressed me the most were the people who worked there—they were so nice! So I got hired, and I've been working there going on seven years. Now I'm the head wench! I'm also artistic director.

"We wait tables, but it's really just feeding people out of a bucket. It's a people job! Unlike a lot of other jobs, where you'd go up onstage, play your role, and then your character disappears with you into the dressing room, we are out among people from the moment they walk in the door.

"As artistic director, I'm trying to have women take a more central role in the show. We're developing more wench characters. There's one wench who's now featured, an opportunist, who has a lot of interaction with the King, and wants to be the Queen. Ultimately, we will have a Queen in the production—the producer, Don Aiken, writes the material.

"There are about six or seven songs in the show. Some are musical comedy production numbers with the entire cast, others are more serious, like 'Scarborough Faire.' There's a minstrel section of the show, where we can really show off our musicianship. I stage the shows mostly. Rehearsals are difficult—we do shows Wednesday through Sunday. We get there at 5:30, and we have to be ready to go at ten after seven. When we get there, we have about an hour to set up the room and rehearse. There are a few times where we had shows that were cancelled, and then we'll get a nice chunk of time to work things out. It's kind of hard because we have a rotating cast, and so we have to teach them new things, and it's hard to keep track of who knows what, and who's done what."

Staying Strong

"At the Medieval Manor, people come in and notice what a great time we're having, and they think our work is easy. We work really hard! There are a lot of things you have to do physically to stay ready for a job like this. I work out at the gym five times a week; I've got to stay in shape. I'm on my feet, running around, dancing, singing. I've got to keep my voice healthy. People think, 'I want to do this job! Do I have to audition?' I say, 'Do you have a picture and resume? Have you ever done professional theater?' They say no. People don't understand that we're all professionals, because it looks fun and effortless. But that's the kind of work I wanna do—I don't want my work to feel like work. I know I'm doing something right when I'm having a blast doing it."

Having It All

"I really love what I do. I'm not a millionaire, but I don't even worry about where my income's coming from, because I know the amount of energy and love I've put into my career guarantees I'll keep working. I could not imagine doing anything else! I have a list of things I've always wanted to do—and I'm chipping away at the list."

SERVICE WITH A SMILE

Ninety-nine point nine percent of all actors who have worked as waiters DON'T want to talk about it. Really, who could blame them? You slave away at long, sweaty shifts, fetching fettucine for rude creeps who barely make eye contact with you, let alone tip sufficiently. And that's on a GOOD day.

Debbie Williams *is* willing to share her trials and tribulations from restaurant purgatory. Williams is not only a former cater-waiter, she turned her experience into the hit one-woman show *Under My Apron*, which played to capacity crowds and great reviews at New York City's 2005 Midtown International Theatre Festival. This sketch show offers funny, true-to-life portraits of drunken, argumentative customers, ego-riddled waitstaff, and not a few poignant moments about wanting more out of life.

Williams trained in classical ballet from the age of four to her teens. She served as artistic director of her brother Barry Hughson's company, The Youth Theatre, and co-owns both Real Arts, the production company behind *Under My Apron*, and a photography company, RealPhotoNY.com, with her husband, Ron. Read on as she makes a few key observations on the work she's done.

People Think Waiters Aren't People

"As an actor, I've had many 'survival' jobs. I've worked in coffee bars, video stores, convention centers. I even had a gig as a magician's assistant! The one job I probably share with most actors is waiting tables, more specifically, cater-waitering. Through cater-waitering, I met so many people: actors, writers, models, artists, and even some career waiters. It was amazing to me that so many people with totally different backgrounds, from all over the country and all over the world, were working this same job.

141

"There's a lot of material to write about right there, but even more interesting sometimes were the people that we waiters, this eclectic group of aspiring 'somethings,' waited on. How when they looked at us, all they saw was a waiter. So that, combined with conversations and dinners out (as a patron myself) were the things that inspired *Under My Apron*."

Writing Is the Best Revenge

"My dad loved to write, so I guess I got the love from him, but much like him, I always wrote but never did anything with it. I just left it on the paper or in the computer. Then, a couple of years ago, my husband and I were feeling in need of a creative outlet. We decided we'd call some of our actor friends who were in town at the time to see if they wanted to do a reading group. I then got the crazy idea to let the group read some of the scenes (for *Under My Apron*) I had written to see how they'd sound. It was a very frightening experience for me. Writing is so personal, but these were my close friends, and all great actors, so somehow I pulled up the courage to let them say my words out loud. Much to my surprise, they were even better out loud than in my head! I know full well this won't happen every time, but hearing those words inspired me to continue to write and continue to hear my words aloud."

Multi-tasking Is All Good

"It's hard for me to pinpoint the most rewarding aspect of *Under My Apron*. I wrote it, I directed it, I performed in it, and with the Midtown International Theatre Festival, I produced it. Too many hats? I don't think so, at least not at this level. When *Under My Apron* is produced in a bigger and more permanent way, then I guess I'll have to make some choices as to what's most fulfilling, and where I'm most beneficial to the piece."

True Pride

"I've performed all over the country and all over the world, and I'm super-proud of all my accomplishments, but *Under My Apron* was a combination of all of my passions, so I was able to experience it on every level. Just the fact that something I wrote was performed by

a professional actors' theater in New York City is amazing to me—
and performed to outstanding reviews! Anything that happens with
Under My Apron in the future is just icing on the cake."

LIFE OF THE PARTY

Sebastian Saraceno loves nothing more than having a good time—
and inspiring others to do the same. As an actor, he's won raves
appearing onstage with Florida's Salerno Theatre Company and has
been featured in films like *Hooligans' Valley* (Other Side Cinemas).
Saraceno's other major forte is a flair for live event entertainment.
He's not only a wildly popular bartender in the Tampa Bay area, he
works through Short Entertainment Productions, as part of a little
person bartending team that does private parties all over the US,
and through Fired Up Entertainment doing additional live events.

Read on to find out how Saraceno's come to ply his hugely
successful skills—which include fire-breathing, by the way:

"I got my first taste of entertaining at Countryside High
School in Clearwater, Florida. The school had a news program that
was televised in the classrooms, doing school announcements. We
would do comedy skits; one of the first I ever did was playing a com-
mando elf who would make sure everyone in school was being good.
If someone was being bad, say stealing food in the lunch line of the
cafeteria, I would throw them in a trash can. I liked that!

"I started really immersing myself in entertainment after high
school. I started doing radio in the Tampa Bay area; one of my
friends from school called me up and wanted me to work on one of
the morning shows, where I did more comedy. I made a lot of contacts, and from there, I went on to bartending, where I got a lot of
exposure, actually. I became a full service bartender, but I also
would entertain, get up on the bar and dance, and I learned how to
fire-breathe. Fire-breathing is definitely hair-raising the first time
you do it, but there is a technique I learned from another bartender
that's safe—and which I'll keep secret! It's now a great gimmick
of mine—everywhere I ever work, from bars to nightclubs, I always
do it.

"With the Salerno Theatre Company, I did *A Funny Thing
Happened on the Way to the Forum*, *Jekyll and Hyde*, and *Damn
Yankees*, in which I played a total of six parts. That show taught me so
much about choreography and character, as I had to switch from

character to character in a matter of seconds. I pulled it off, and it was so challenging, but so fulfilling. It was incredible too, because as I'm a little person, roles are often stereotyped: a jester, an elf, a circus performer, or whatever. But the cool thing about this theater company was that the directors thought outside of the box. They cast me in roles written for average-sized people, and there was not one mention made about my height.

"I love theater. That's why I love doing live entertainment—in bartending, you use flair, flipping the bottles around like Tom Cruise in *Cocktail*, or you wait till the right moment in a dark club, and breathe a fireball! The crowd starts screaming, and I'm a kid in a candy store.

"In terms of building up my brand in the nightclub business, I've worked all over the country. Bars and nightclubs come and go; they'll stay open for a year or two, then they close. So I would stay with a bar for about a year, then move on to another bar, the average exodus every bartender usually makes. But my first year of bartending, I actually met an agent, who saw me and gave me his business card. I got my head shots done, and was able to make more contacts [through him]. In bartending, interpersonal relations are incredibly important. Your personality is the biggest tool you have.

"Locally, I'd work Thursday, Friday, and Saturday. Bartending takes a lot out of you physically; I'd wake up around 2 PM, work out, and be into work by eight or nine o'clock. I'd be slammed with customers; bartending's not just a job where you have a good time, you've got to run around and hustle, to the point where you're sweating like you've run a marathon. The bars in Florida close around 2 AM, and then you clean up, count your money, and get out of the bar around 3:30. I lived about an hour away, so I wouldn't get home till 4:30, and then your brain is so stimulated, between ten or twelve drink recipes in your head and having people yell orders to you all night, you're wired. It takes a while to calm down; I wouldn't be able to go to sleep until six or seven in the morning.

"This is something that I also did back in the day; you get an entertainment gig and get really excited about it, thinking, ooh, this is gonna be my big break. Then it doesn't happen. I would do any tiny little gig and think, this could lead to my making a million dollars! But in order to progress in your acting career, you've got to do a lot of things for free.

"I usually travel around the country about three to four times a month for gigs. Sometimes, I travel somewhere and come back the same day! Say they'll want me somewhere on a Sunday. I'll be getting off a bartending shift and going straight to the airport, and won't even go to bed. For one gig in San Jose, I had to bartend on a Saturday night—we were slammed, of course—and I got out late, changed my clothes, jumped in my car, went straight to the airport and onto a plane. I did the gig, lots of singing and dancing, on Sunday, got back on a plane, and was home in Florida on Sunday night. It's a four- to five-hour plane ride each way; you have those kind of days. Since I really love everything I'm doing, I don't mind missing a day of sleep.

"My most memorable gig so far? The Maxim Magazine Super Bowl Party in Nashville. That was incredible. I met Jim McMahon, my football hero, and as I was a football player myself, that made my day. I dressed up as Mini-Elvis for that gig; I had a good old time, got up onstage with the band, and sang some Bon Jovi. It was so cool.

"I've been working for about eight years. You have to have a stable income, so you can pay your bills and not go broke, and at the same time, have to learn how to sacrifice your spare time to ultimately do what you want to do in life, to pursue an acting career in the future. I'm an incredibly ambitious person. I'll stop at nothing to at least be semi-successful. I say that because what acting all boils down to is, you can create every condition right in order to succeed, but if you don't have a little bit of luck and good timing, sometimes it doesn't happen. Ultimately, I'd also love to own my own bar, restaurant or nightclub."

eleven
hitting the right notes

When an actor seeking a new career sits down to outline his or her physical skill set, honed musical/vocal technique often emerges as a significant strength. From a commercial standpoint, this is a major plus. In the business world, there are a surprisingly large number of positions that require an ability to "hit the right notes," either through actually singing and playing an instrument, being able to employ an ear for accents, or create a specific vocal effect at the drop of a hat. These jobs pay off, both financially and emotionally.

The actors-turned-businessfolk in this chapter have figured out precisely how they can market their pitch-perfect talents in ways that benefit both society AND business. The work that they do differs from Bob Bergen's animation voice-over work or Laura Giannelli's book-on-tape narration efforts (as outlined in chapter 8) because it's less character-driven and more situational—to serve

147

a specific client, project, or larger purpose. That said, the people you are about to learn from are true artists with tremendous creative integrity. This is how they accomplish a day's work.

SIGNS OF SUCCESS

Lora Heller's son Zeke helped start a revolution at only six-and-a-half months old. A former actress and board certified music therapist who holds an MS in special education/deaf education, Heller was thrilled when Zeke actually began to use American Sign Language, under her influence, at such a young age. Inspired to help other children out of this experience, Heller founded Baby Fingers, a New York City-based organization that teaches both signing and music to babies, toddlers, older kids, and their parents. Both hearing children and deaf children happily participate in, and benefit from, Heller's program, which began in 2000.

Heller's creative talent blossomed in her childhood. "I always liked to sing, and realized it was fun when people were watching," she recalls. "As kids, my sister and I would put on little shows for each other, or together for our parents. We would sing along to the *Grease* movie soundtrack with John Travolta and Olivia Newton-John, and act out the parts. In elementary school, I always enjoyed acting out our class stories, and being involved in summer camp plays. Being onstage gave me a high—it became a magical, yet safe and comfortable, place."

Her heartfelt compassion for others was also apparent very early on, when as a fourteen-year-old summer camp counselor, Heller learned to sign so that she could communicate with a deaf camper. In college, her thesis was a stage production performed simultaneously in English and in ASL; it was extremely well-received. "I wrote, directed and produced a musical play which included significant issues facing college students—it incorporated deaf actors, and there was sign language during all the songs. It was a fully therapeutic and educational experience for performers and audience alike," Heller says. Her subsequent graduate sequence encompassed a pilot program, which imparted both ASL and music to kids from age three months to three years.

Heller's love of the limelight stayed with her. "I continued to perform—in summer stock, in college, in professional theater," she remembers. In fact, while practicing music therapy in Rochester,

New York, after finishing school, Heller enjoyed a busy dual career as an in-demand actress in the Big Apple. "I especially liked to perform shows for kids, and I found that I loved directing children's theater. The opportunity to see a love of performing in the children with whom I worked, and to assist in developing their skills as well as their self-esteem, was always rewarding and gratifying. I learned a lot from the children—pure innocence onstage was always inspiring. I love to see an audience respond to music as well, and feel proud to give them an opportunity to laugh, cry, and reflect."

Heller offered music therapy, music classes, educational enrichment, drama workshops, and sign language courses at many prestigious facilities, including the New York School for the Deaf, St. Mary's Hospital, St. Luke's Hospital, and the 92nd Street Y, all in Manhattan. Then Zeke's sign language achievement inspired her to create Baby Fingers: "My philosophy (was) simple. I wanted to be sure to provide creative arts experiences and education while improving communication and language development."

Heller's approach combines music (she sings and plays guitar with her students) and ASL as a comprehensive curriculum. She points to significant research that shows babies who sign have a stronger command of verbal language, and start talking at a younger age than babies who do not have sign language exposure and instruction. The reaction to her work from both kids and parents has been wildly positive. "I feel so fulfilled by the response to my music, sign language, and overall interactions in my classes," Heller exalts. "When a mom says, 'He signed "milk" yesterday!', or a toddler approaches to strum the guitar with me, or a baby claps for the first time during a song—my work day is complete!"

Another huge benefit for Heller is that she feels having her own company helps her achieve balance between her job and her family life. (She is now the mom of her second child, Sian.) A typical Monday in her life:

Early morning: Heller gets her two kids ready, then both she and her husband walk them to school—a bit of family time.

Morning into afternoon: Heller starts her workday at a therapeutic preschool in a local hospital: her music therapy work here includes active music-making, movement to music, sign language, and overall developmental support for children with a variety of special needs. From there, Heller heads to a local children's center, where she teaches Baby Fingers sign language and music to a group of moms with developing babies and toddlers. Heller then plunges into a one-on-one music therapy session with a six-year-old boy with autism.

Later that afternoon: She picks up her kids, and puts her mom hat back on.

Evening: One evening a week, Heller either attends an informal sign language group, meets with her faculty, trains professionals working with children who may need sign language, or gives a presentation on Baby Fingers.

The timing works out very well. "I have the flexibility to set my own on-site work schedule, so that I can be a part of my children's daily schedules and activities," Heller says. "My children also participate in Baby Fingers and other work events when appropriate—they often enjoy being a part of a music therapy group or a sign language lesson."

Heller is delighted with the contributions made through Baby Fingers, and her achievements just keep piling up (she's also the author of three very well-received books on sign language). "It took a lot to get that first class off the ground; in five and a half years, it went from a one woman show to a company with a faculty!" Overall, Heller's admirable accomplishments afford her both deep professional pride and the joy of knowing she's made the world a better place. As she puts it, "In my mind, being successful professionally means to be happy at work. So I feel successful. I also feel lucky that I can make a difference in the lives of others through my work."

THE DIALOGUE GURU

Constantine Gregory's performance resume is packed with roles in scores of films, including *Golden Eye, The Sum of All Fears, The Russia House*, and many, many more. He's been directed by the likes of Julie Taymor, Bernardo Bertolucci, Peter Brook, and Blake Edwards. Equally impressive as this London-based virtuoso's acting credentials is his stellar experience as a dialogue coach for films including *The Last Emperor, Mission: Impossible, Birthday Girl, The Peacemaker*, and *The Dreamers*, to name just a few. Gregory has dialogue-coached some of the most respected actors in the business, such as Tom Cruise, Nicole Kidman, George Clooney, Anthony Hopkins, Jessica Lange, Kenneth Branagh, Keanu Reeves, Sean Connery, and Peter O' Toole.

In addition to being so very gifted at the work he does, the good-natured Mr. Gregory is happy to share his story of the road that brought him from falling in love with cinema in a darkened theater to becoming one of its most crucial architects.

"I always acted, from my very earliest days. I would make up plays, get friends involved, and so forth. At school, I was always in productions, as well as doing my own things. I started a film club at school, because I was so keen on film. It was also a way of seeing films rated above our age, as clubs did not fall under censorship rules. As a teenager, during the holidays in London (I was at boarding school), I went to the movies almost every day, sometimes two and even three times a day. Kurosawa, Antonioni, Truffaut, Bergman . . . as well as more commercial movies. I went to the theater frequently, and loved it. I saw all these plays and films, these great productions with truly amazing actors—and it NEVER occurred to me that I might do it myself.

"It was only at university, at Trinity College in Dublin, when I joined the Dramatic Society (which performed plays which ran for two weeks every term for the public) that the penny finally dropped. This is what I wanted to do, not banking, which is why I was studying economics!

"When I graduated, I only knew one person in the business, a theater producer. He gave me my first job, as the back legs of a horse in a Christmas show. I also understudied the lead, *Toad of Toad Hall*.

"Because I speak Russian, and in those days movies were made with Russian baddies, I got into films relatively early on. Russian baddies became foreign baddies, as I have always had a facility with accents, being able to do them completely naturally. Over time, British parts came my way, and fewer baddies. There was theater, too. After the traditional beginning in fortnightly repertory theater in the provinces, I was at the Royal Shakespeare Company. I worked with the great Jean-Louis Barrault in London, performed at the Royal Court.

"Because I could do accents, I got work in re-voicing films. All films need additional voices recorded in post-production. This is known as 'looping', or ADR (automated dialogue replacement). Without going into technical detail, when a scene is shot with people in the background, those extras mime speaking, and voices are put on in the recording studio later. This is done so that there is complete control over the recording of the principal characters' dialogue during the shooting. There are also multi-national films, shot in England, where the smaller roles are played by non-English-speaking actors, and if their accents are inappropriate, or too heavy, they will be re-voiced by English-speaking actors. I worked quite regularly in this, as a second string to my acting bow, joining a friend who had started a company which specialized in casting and supplying voices.

"We were approached by a casting director who asked if we knew anyone who might be able to dialogue-coach a TV movie filmed in then-Yugoslavia. I thought I wouldn't mind having a go, met the producers and director, and somehow convinced them I was the right person. It was about the life of Mussolini, starring George C. Scott, Lee Grant, the late, wonderful Raul Julia, Virginia Madsen, the gorgeous Mary Elizabeth Mastrantonio in her first film, a young Gabriel Byrne, and an even-younger Robert Downey, Jr. Other main parts were played by English actors, and the minor roles were played by Yugoslav actors, well-known in their country, drawn from the National Theatre.

"The brief was that all would speak with a slight Italian accent. A couple of days after I arrived in Zagreb, I met George C. Scott, and asked this formidable man how much of an accent he planned to use, as I would use him as a model. 'I ain't speaking in no f-ing accent!', the bear growled. So the brief became to help all the British actors with American accents, and the Yugoslavs to speak as clearly as possible.

"I immediately fell in love with the work. Being an actor myself, and I believe I am the only dialogue coach who is also an actor, was invaluable, as I knew exactly what the actors were going through. I grew to understand the degree to which confidence plays a part, far more than the emphasis on clear enunciation or phonetic tricks.

"One thing led to another, and I found myself soon after in Beijing working on *The Last Emperor*, directed by the great Bernardo Bertolucci. My brief was to unify the way everyone spoke. English represented Chinese, so everyone had to speak fluidly, as if they were speaking their native tongue. The actors came from all over the world, and from mainland China. No two actors spoke English in the same way or with the same accent, so I devised a manner of speech they could all do, and they would all sound as though they inhabited the same world. To my great pleasure, in all of the success of that film, the way people spoke was NEVER commented on. In fact, a very knowledgeable film critic in England referred to *The Last Emperor* as one of the few foreign language films (!) to have won an Oscar.

"I do not think of myself as successful. Great things were predicted for me as an actor by many people, and I would have wished for more constant employment in bigger roles. My dream had always been to be a leading supporting actor. They have all the best parts, all the fun, without the burden of stardom. That I have made a living, been the sole support of my family, is certainly a kind of success, and I am proud of my reputation as a dialogue coach. You need passion for your work. As a dialogue coach, you need great diplomatic skills to deal with the director and the actors, the ability to improvise and adapt, as no two films, no two briefs, no two actors, are the same. Each is a new challenge, and I'm grateful I haven't been found out yet.

"[When considering moving from acting to other work] be open to anything. Most actors need to supplement their incomes by doing other jobs. Most actors have people skills, and most find that they do part-time work very well; first, because they know it isn't forever, and secondly, because they can play the role of chauffeur or decorator or even office worker very well.

"As a coach, every job has been a success, in that I have succeeded, and sometimes even exceeded, in what I was given to do. Ultimately, success is for the work not to be noticed, and most importantly, that the actors with whom I have worked feel free to ACT well.

"It's heaven, as far as I'm concerned. I must have done something very right in a past life."

SMOOTH OPERATOR

Jill Perry's mellifluous voice has been heard in countless radio and TV spots; her clients have included Ford and the American Cancer Society. Working out of Georgia for companies nationwide for commercials, web-based tutorials and more, Perry's uncanny ability to capture and/or create whatever vocal effect a job may call for has marked her as the best in the talent marketplace. She's also extremely wise about managing her business. Here, she lets us in on her successful work strategy.

153

Q: Talk about how you started acting, first of all.

A: I was a junior in college when I discovered stage acting. There just wasn't anything else I was that interested in. At my state university in Georgia, I was the first person to take an acting degree out the door, and I just ran with it! Out of school, I started acting professionally right off the bat. Living twenty minutes outside of Atlanta, there's a number of Shakespeare theaters, and a great opportunity to do classic things, or modern things.

Q: So then how did voicing commercials come into play?

A: Since I was fifteen, I've always had a job—usually involving sales in some way. So in addition to acting, I also worked for Macy's at a cosmetics counter. In that job, you have to be able to talk to people, and touch people. I went on to become a freelance makeup artist for five, seven different cosmetics companies at the same time, to make ends meet so I could act for nothing.

   I had a friend, Freddy Taylor, that I made when I attended Georgia State University back in 1988 for one year. He was a great guy, came down from Philly to attend film school, and he said to me, "You have a great voice! You should do voice-overs." So I tried to do a voice-over for him, and he said, "You sound like a schoolteacher—it's supposed to sound more commercial." But years later, Freddy had his own production company, and his partner called me up and said, "We have this commercial—would you like to do the voice-over for it?" I said, "Sure, I'll do it for free." It would be fun, and would get me familiar with being in a studio. So I drove to Atlanta, and at the studio, they handed me the copy. The job was for some sort of blood analysis company. It was good copy, but when they played me the underlying music, that's when it all clicked. Its ambience was very Enya-like, and that's how I got the right vibe. Plus I had a good director. So that launched me—I thought, maybe I can figure out how to get into this business.

Q: So how did you take the next step?

A: I talked to a woman named Cher Guthrie, who used to teach voice-over and acting classes at a local studio, and asked if I could audit a class. Afterward, she and I sat down and pored over four or five magazines, tore out seven or eight ads, and she said, "OK, take these, and work on them." We went to another studio, she directed me, her husband mixed seven tracks down into a minute-and-a-half voice-over demo. I sent it out to eight agencies here in Atlanta, and one agent would talk to me, Kathy Hardegree of Atlanta Models and Talent. She's an amazing woman; she knows her stuff. I took a contract home, and a union handbook.

Nothing happened for a year, I cried my eyes out. I thought I was losing my mind. But then, the jobs started, and they've never stopped since 1997. Once I bought a house and put a studio in my home, and put a Web site up, the world just blew up.

The Internet really put this whole career in my lap. It's amazing! I never dreamt this big. I know we're taught to dream big, but it's pretty scary to really do it. You have to have a lust for life; you have to talk to everybody about the work you want to do, although not to the point of annoying them, and tell them what you're about.

Most voice-over artists go to Los Angeles. In 2002, I went out and talked to ICM, because they're the biggest and the best. They had heard my stuff and liked it, through the ad agency WestWayne. At that time, they had three women who sounded just like me, though, so they couldn't sign me, and I thought, without a guarantee, without representation, I'm going to go home. Because, you know, it's pretty neat to be able to stay in your city, establish a career, and have people know who you are. Local people to me are my roots—it's all about networking. I've met really fabulous people who've enabled me to do some really great things for ad agencies. It's all about persistence.

Q: What the process like when you work with an ad agency to do a commercial?

A: Here's a how to work with an ad agency. Say the booking comes from one of your agents (voice-over artists often have several)—you're on their roster, and your demo is on their Web site. They'll have an ad agency person writing scripts for a specific company, and this agency person will pick four female voices, and want all four to read the copy. This used to be done in person; now we can do this remotely.

When I get the copy, the first thing I do is research the client. Let's say I'm working for a firearms company. Who are they? What's their Web site look like? Is this job for television or radio? What parts of the country is it going to play in? If I can find these things out, I will, because if it's playing in the midwest to a bunch of farmers, that's different than if it's playing for Jaguar-driving, high-falutin' guys who like to shoot on the weekends. I try to find out who my audience is.

I also try to find out what kind of branding the ad agency is looking for. Is this going to be a 360-degree change from what they've done in previous years, or is this just the new campaign, and they're trying it with a female voice? Because who expects a female to be talking about firearms? So I find that out.

Now I start to think about interpretation. Are they going to want something really specific? I look at the directions they give me—usually, online, I'll get one copy of the script, and another page of specs—'We want a female, age thirty to fifty', or 'We want a conversational type', or 'We want a very strict announcer type', or 'We want a warm and friendly sound.' I'll put down two or three different takes. Then they'll decide if my voice is going to suit their purpose best. If it doesn't, I can't take it personally.

So if I win the audition, they say, be at such-and-such a place at such-and-such a time on Tuesday. I show up ten minutes before that time. You've always got to be prompt, smiling, and happy no matter what's going on in your life, with a bottle of water. You check in, walk into the studio, and meet the ad guys, one or two writers. Sometimes the client is there, too, but that's a perk, because most of the time the client is just waiting for the ad guy to call with the finished product.

The engineer is your best friend—he can make you sound your best. When everyone's ready, I step in front of the microphone, put the copy on the music stand in front of me, put the headphones on, look through the glass and smile and wave. Then we start rollin'. Usually I'll go through the copy for the whole spot once, then I'll be given feedback. Sometimes, though, I'll be told at the top, 'What we're looking for is like what you did in your track, but can you make it smilier? We want to hear more smile in your voice.' It's a full-body acting job. It's pretty physical, and there's a lot of emotional interpretation.

Q: It sounds like it's important to be able to think on your feet.

A: Thinking on your feet in this job is essential. Every agent wants something from you either in the next five minutes or in the last five minutes. Sometimes people will forget to check their messages from over the weekend, so they call you late and you've got to deliver it now. You've got to be able to figure out how to make the situation positive and communicate that effectively to whoever's asking for something from you.

Q: What kind of common-sense business advice would you give aspiring voice-over artists?

A: I think I've always had a very responsible, tight-fisted side. I don't want to owe anybody anything. My dad very practically made me put half of everything I made as a kid away in a savings account. I wish schools would draw a clear line for artistic students, and say, 'All right, you can be as creative as you want to be, but this is the business course you have to take—you have to be able to handle your own finances.' You have to stay straight with the tax man. You have to put your 401K together yourself with your accountant. These are all things I've had to learn to figure out to do along the way.

Also, I've had agents communicate very abrasively with me, and that's just sent me to another agent. Your agent works for you! You're paying HIM! He's not doing anything but opening the door for you. Yeah, that's essential, but you don't owe him an arm and a leg. There should be an equal, kind relationship, where you communicate kindly, and give 100 percent to each other.

Q: What's the best part of doing this job for you?

A: It's very demanding, but it's also very rewarding if it's what you want to do, and you find that out after a few good years in the trenches!

twelve
express yourself

"Organic." It's a word I heard over and over again when talking

with the actors whose stories you've been reading in this book.

Look it up in the dictionary, and you'll find its meaning comes from

the power contained inside a living force. To great actors every-

where, the definition of "organic" is vitally important, because the

strength of an actor's mind and body are obviously his/her most

essential tools in interpreting a role. Plus, REALLY smart actors

also totally get the fact that using their organic selves in other out-

of-the-box alternate work situations can bring you success, and

a fat income.

The actors profiled in this chapter have found unique ways to work purely with their bodies and brains within their alternate career choices. It's a pretty savvy strategy when you think about it: to make money, you don't need to invest start-up cash, or master fancy computer equipment. You just have to use your arms, legs, brains, and common sense. Read on to find out how they do it.

STREET LIFE

Every morning, Robert John Burck gets up at the crack of dawn at the Royal Motel in Secaucus, New Jersey. He starts his day reading motivational books for three to four hours, then heads to the gym for an intense eliptical machine workout, all to reach the state of "peak emotional intensity" he needs to ace his workday. Burck then goes back to the Royal, puts on a pair of cowboy boots, underpants, and a cowboy hat—and that's all. He grabs his guitar, jumps into his car, and drives to a midtown parking garage in Manhattan. He parks, and swaggers to the turf he calls his own—Times Square. There, no matter what the weather, until darkness falls, he plays his self-written music, poses for photographs with eager passersby, and lives out his legend as the world's most successful street performer. He is the Naked Cowboy.

Burck started out with no connections, but loads of self-belief, and it's paying off in a big way. He's made personal appearances everywhere from Florida to California to Japan, has appeared on scores of TV shows, done radio like *The Howard Stern Show*, and even attended the United Nations Millennium Conference. Sponsors such as Calvin Klein, Flycell, and Icon Parking are lining up; his image sells ring tones, guitars, CDs, and comic books. Here he outlines his career track with great confidence, intelligence, and good humor:

"About eleven years ago, I read a book called *Unlimited Power* by Anthony Robbins. I was a troubled adolescent from Cincinnati, Ohio, doing anything to get attention, no direction to my life, and no role models. I literally read that book thirty-six times straight—going through it, writing goals, financial, social, sociological. The coolest goal I could think of was, I wanted to be king of the earth, period.

"Somebody just said to me one day, 'Why don't you become a stripper?' So I started working in that field, if you will, for a short time, while I was going to college in Cincinnati. I did love the attention; I worked out all the time, so I was all into looking good. Someone else said, 'Why don't you become a model?' Now, being a model was cooler than being a stripper, in my point of view. So I figured, I was such a beautiful guy, they'd throw me in all the magazines, and then I'd heard stories of people who'd been in magazines who were put into movies. So then I'd be a movie star, the highest goal I could think of next to being president of the United States.

"I started commuting between Cincinnati and California. I would send modeling head shots around everywhere, and people would call me just to say I had no idea what I was doing, I was going about modeling wrong. And of course, the other thing I kind of forgot was, in order to be a movie star, I would have to know how to act. So I did a couple of plays around my hometown. But basically, my thing was, I want to be a star right this minute! I didn't want to wait and take acting classes and all that crap; I knew I was beautiful, I knew I was the coolest guy in the world. I knew I could do anything I put my mind to.

"I read many books on acting, philosophy. Anthony Robbins suggests finding someone who did what you want to do and model them, so I read lots of biographies, too. But there was no biography written that had what I wanted, because I wanted to surpass and level Elvis, Madonna, Donald Trump, and Bill Clinton. I wanted to do nothing but give love to people through our media culture.

"I was in Venice Beach in 1998, shooting for *Playgirl* magazine. Somebody'd just called me out of the blue, and I got the job. I was playing guitar on the boardwalk, just looking for an audience to maybe draw some attention during the shoot, and I was ignored the entire day. The photographer suggested I play in my underwear the following day, and I made over $100 from people passing by! So then I started going city to city, playing guitar in my underwear. I did it in my hometown and was arrested, but got on the news. I did it from Cincinnati all the way to California and back.

"Things started to happen. I was on the street in New York playing one day, and Alec Baldwin jumped out of a car, and ran over to get a picture with me. Then Britney Spears stopped and said, 'Hey! Naked Cowboy!' like I'm her big brother or something, after I've been looking at her on billboards. On MTV, Justin Timberlake pointed out the window, down to Times Square where I was playing, and said, 'That's the hardest-working man in the entertainment business.' Now I see people wearing Naked Cowboy T-shirts; they bring me Naked Cowboy action figures. I got e-mails on Halloween from people who dressed up in THEIR boots and underwear. I'm getting indoctrinated into the culture; seeing the fulfillment of the goals I wrote out years ago, that I would dominate the commercial landscape of the entire

161

world, create an archetype, that the commercial stage would be dominated by one man, one desperado, who would change the way we all look at things.

"Man lives to create hero archetypes. Without those kinds of societal symbols, people would think it was just birth and death. You've got to stretch those boundaries and create those things, or just live like everybody else, in the herd, which I'm just not capable of doing.

"The only obstacle I feel I've yet to overcome, which I'm working on every day, is immortality. I know, without question, that this life is never going to end, and I will be here forever. Everything else—money, relationships—it's all part of the scenery. I believe I'm an immortal being, and while I'm alive, will convey that confidence to the rest of the world."

Yes, it's obvious; Burck is truly one of a kind. His carefully crafted alter ego reveals he's got a real flair for innovative marketing—and in terms of where he takes his brand next—the sky's the limit.

THE COLOR AND THE SHAPE

Performance/multimedia artist Shannon Kringen has always felt free to pursue her passions, wherever they might take her. Kringen is not only an influential spoken word artist, she shows her artwork at a Seattle gallery each month, maintains a popular multimedia Web site (*www.kringgoddess.com*) and has hosted her own public access TV show "GoddessKRING" since 1995. To make a living, she also decided to become a figure model for artists and photographers—and finds this work as satisfying as any other artistic accomplishment.

Why? "I think the way I was raised AND the nature I was born with makes me who I am today—I was born with a sensitivity to color, shape, and sound," Kringen explains. The daughter of a visual artist mom and composer/musician/writer dad, she was encouraged creatively as a kid. "I'm an only child, and remember playing for long periods in my room, singing and dancing and pretending I had my own show, and an audience who wanted to listen to me," she recalls. Kringen and her mother briefly moved to Evolution Art Institute, an art commune in Petaluma, California, when she was nine: "I was exposed to painting, drawing, wood-working, silk-screening, metalsmithing and an overall sense of community."

Kringen first became actively involved in live performance in high school, becoming known for a stunning impersonation of Mick Jagger while lip-synching Rolling Stones music. She then went on to study graphic design, fine art, and painting at college. After she got out of school, Kringen's artistic expertise, love of the limelight, and need to support herself unexpectedly blossomed into an alternate career.

"I kind of fell into figure modeling," she recalls. "I have always loved being photographed, but until my early twenties, was too shy to try modeling. A female friend of mine took some snapshots of me in 1991, when I was twenty-two. They turned out so well that I showed them to a professional fine art photographer who was looking for a model. We worked together on black and white nudes; I then used these shots to start a portfolio. I began working with other photographers. At this same time, I began experimenting with some exotic dancing and began figure modeling for all the colleges around Seattle, as well as for private art groups who hire models."

Kringen quickly found she could book all the gigs she could handle. "One thing I love about figure modeling is the stability of it," she explains. "Models are always paid, whereas fine artists sometimes struggle to sell their work. Being a model is partly a practical decision. I can be around creative, positive energy and earn a living!"

It's also rewarding work emotionally. "I feel a strong sense of purpose being a model. [The artists] need me! They appreciate me!" she exclaims. The work can be physically taxing, but Kringen clearly relishes the many ways she utilizes her gift for movement. "I love to be quiet and still and go into a trance-like state when I do long poses. I also love short-action 'gesture' poses—they are like a form of dance. I'm very body-oriented and love to express out through my poses. I'm more shy with my voice—but very relaxed with my body."

Although figure modeling is a heavily creative endeavor, Kringen stresses the importance of maintaining a professional approach to job seeking. "I have business cards I hand out to anyone who asks me about my work," she says. "I find people online to collaborate on projects with. I spend time each day thinking about what I want to achieve, I focus on that inside my head, and I take action. I have built a modeling career in Seattle by calling and e-mailing everyone I can find who might need a model. I look on art supply store bulletin boards, and Web sites that allow me to post my profile."

Kringen's efforts have started to gain her fame within the art world, as well as in the naturist community, and new work opportunities are continually opening up for her. "I'm amazed I'm able to make my full living from being a figure model/multimedia artist! The part that excites me most about my career is the synchronicity. The traveling opportunities and positive feedback I get from my work feeds me," she enthuses. She has made appearances at naturist events in France, England, Massachusetts, and Florida, based on her status as a well-known life model. Her art career continues to expand as well: not only is her TV show a big public access hit, but singer Tori Amos recently wore a pair of shoes she painted in concert, and acknowledged Kringen from the stage.

Kringen's fruitful take on both art and business marks her as the very model of a modern self-made success story. "I'm fascinated by the possibilities of what we all can create in our lives. Reality is a lot more flexible than some would have us believe. It's important not to let anyone discourage you from following your dreams, and from trusting your internal drive."

THE PROFESSIONAL EXTRA'S SURVIVAL GUIDE

Randy Farias has a slew of illustrious acting credits under his belt. Classically trained at the Royal Academy of Dramatic Art in London, he's interpreted many of the Bard's great characters onstage, plus won great reviews in scores of contemporary dramas and musicals, and worked as a choreographer. He's also found steady, profitable employment as a professional movie extra based in New England. Here he describes his unique adventures in the screen trade, and offers lots of smart advice for those who might appreciate the benefits of blending in behind Brad Pitt's right earlobe.

It's Not All About You

"When doing extra work, the most important thing to remember is that it's extra work. It won't launch you into a starring role, but if you're working with a good director it is still an important job. If you're a good actor, you're still a character at all times, even if you're just eating, walking, or roller skating in the background. If you're there to try to get seen by the camera, you're there for the wrong reason. And if you try to be seen, cause a distraction, or pull focus from the main actor or action, it will be the last film you ever do."

"All films are a lot of hurry-up-and-wait. Lights need to be adjusted, sets moved or fixed, direction given. If you're smart, you'll watch the main actors to see how they prepare for a scene. Note their lack of expansive gestures and volume, as opposed to a theater performance. Note the technical method of acting necessary to match a wideshot with a closeup. Extra work is a great study opportunity."

Start Likin' the Money

"I think extra work is great financially, at least if you're in the union. The pay is similar to an average wage, and there is overtime, double time, and even 'Golden Time,' when after a certain amount of hours, each hour is a full day's pay. Plus, there's meal penalties, extra pay if you use your own car, wet pay, smoke pay, light stunt pay, and other beneficial moneymaking perks. In the case of the film *The Crucible*, I had to drive out to a production office on a separate day from shooting and have a special fitting for my costume, since I was to play a higher-class puritan citizen in Salem than other extras; being union, I was paid for my time."

See What the Day Brings

"A typical workday: I sign in at my call time, which is usually very early on most films, with someone who checks me off as being on time, and gives me a voucher to sign, and usually I have to fill out W-4/I-9 forms. I report to wardrobe, where, if I was told to bring my own wardrobe, they check to make sure it's appropriate, or they give you wardrobe. Then, makeup and hair—

165

depending on the type of film I'm doing, this can be very involving. The first film I ever worked on was the TV movie *The Kennedys of Massachusetts*—I was in several scenes set during the thirties and forties. They cut everyone's hair, in this mass production hair room, and they just mangled it. I ended up with this hideous 'do, a half pageboy, half bowl cut, and then they drenched it with Vaseline to paste it to the side of my head and gave me a big wide part down the middle. It was so hideous, I kid you not, I met the boyfriend of a woman who worked on the movie four years later, and he remembered me as 'the guy with that ugly hairdo in the movie.'

"After wardrobe, make-up, and hair, I head onto set, where we extras are told what 'action' we're supposed to be doing in the scene—if a cheer, laughter, or some other sort of response is needed. If you're one of only a few extras, it's a dream, because it often means getting to work with the main cast members. On *Housesitter* I had about four days on set with Steve Martin and Goldie Hawn, playing a caterer in a party scene; there were only about four extras at first, so for a week I got to watch and really learn from those actors and from Frank Oz, the director."

Let Caution Be Your Guide

"Some things, you definitely want to be careful about. In *The Crucible*, I wore a costume that I was told was worth three thousand dollars. Now, this made a huge difference in terms of what I could and could not do on set; if I ate anything, I'd have to take it all off, for example. In the same film, the township was supposed to have really dirty, rotten-looking teeth. The makeup people were always rubbing our teeth with spirit gum and brown makeup—and using the same swab in everyone's mouth! It was so unsanitary and gross, I went out and bought a package of crayons, and would just scribble all over my teeth, till they looked horrid. When a makeup woman came over with her disease brush, I'd just smile and say, 'They already did me.' "

See the Big Picture

"Overall, I've had many creative and critical successes in my career, of which I'm very proud. But all the good reviews in the world cannot buy you a house, or pay rent, or food, or doctor's bills. Film is where the money really lies. To me, true professional success is to just act, and know that I'm making enough for health insurance, to pay the bills and have a little savings. I don't need to be rich, and I don't need to be a star, just a constantly working actor doing good projects."

thirteen
industry insiders

When many actors think about career change, their first goal is to try to stay working in the entertainment industry however possible. This is sometimes the right move, and sometimes not.

First, the tough reality: arts-related jobs are tremendously hard to come by. Many administrative slots in arts organizations are already filled by professionals with some sort of performance background themselves; these folks tend to latch on like barnacles to their positions for years, which is quite understandable. On the bright side, though, if you CAN find a position that utilizes the hard-earned creative skills you've developed—great emotional intelligence and people-savvy, an innate understanding of the way the business of show business works, and the know-how to collaborate well with fellow artists—you're probably gonna love going to work in the morning.

The success stories spotlighted within this chapter show you the fruits of entertainment industry–related labor. Each of the following pros shares one essential quality: the desire to advocate for others. They are generous with their wisdom, and dedicated to getting the word out about the wonderful work the folks they work with are capable of. Talk about a truly worthwhile day's work!

THE PROVOCATIVE PUBLICIST

Deb Pickman knows how to get her message across. A co-founder of the trailblazing, Vancouver-based theater, music, film, and visual arts collective Shameless Hussy Productions, Pickman devoted her acting career to artistic rebellion, telling provocative feminist stories. (A Jessie Richardson nominee, Pickman's resume with Shameless Hussy includes *Sonofabitch Stew: the drunken life of Calamity Jane*, *Bonnie Dangerously; fast times with that guy Clyde*, and *My Left Breast*.)

Now she's focused her energies significantly on public relations, and is fiercely dedicated to helping emerging artists from all mediums get their work seen and heard. Here's how Pickman formed her plan of action:

"I think like a lot of people, I thought about acting when I was growing up, but it seemed like a fantasy. I followed another career path until I was about twenty-eight—I was working in retail and wholesale ladieswear. Then I took a personal development course. I'd never done anything like that before, and was skeptical, just because I hadn't done it, I suppose. But I went ahead and tried it, and it really did open up a lot of things for me. I got some feedback that suggested I was a lot more powerful than I thought I was in different areas, and I did go on to do a little more personal development work. What it all came down to for me was getting in touch with something that each of us has to give, and that nobody else can give on the planet. Tuning into that really brings juice to life, and a thrill and excitement. So I just got the idea to try acting—looking back, it seems so unrealistic, but I'm so glad I did it!

"The first time I was ever in a real production, I remember going to my opening night and thinking, 'If I survive this, I'll never do it again!' If you feel there's so much to risk, though, it really heightens the achievement. So I went back to school, and got my degree in theater from the University of British Columbia—it was so wonderful! Then one girlfriend I'd met in school, Renee Iaci, and I did summer stock together, and had gotten really into the hard work of producing a play. It was exciting to us to see how you could write a press release, send it out to the media, and people would actually come to your show. When I look back now, I see that was when I started to really fold in the kinds of skills that I'd already been developing for ten years in sales. I see now that I'd finally found something I believed in to sell.

"We started Shameless Hussy Productions together in 1992, after graduation, with another friend, Lana Krause, a costume designer. My wonderful husband, John Baker, who's in the personal development field, too, and works with corporations, helped us focus on a mandate. (Like my mom, Johnny pretty much promised me that I could do anything I set my mind to.) We basically at first just wanted an opportunity for people to see our work. We came out with the mandate, 'Telling provocative stories about women, to inspire the hand that rocks the cradle to rock the world.' I had no idea that I was a feminist until then, but my whole life has been folded into the pursuit of that mandate in many ways.

"When I first started doing publicity (for Shameless Hussy), I found it terrifying. I think part of the challenge was that I was inviting reviewers to come, encouraging them by saying it was going to be the best thing they'd ever seen, and it was up to me onstage to deliver on my promise. There was nowhere to hide! But because I believed in what we were doing so much, I just dug in and did it. Two friends in particular, knowing I was operating on a shoestring budget with our young company, told me, 'Publicity would be a great day job for you!' Brian, one of my friends who'd said this to me, ended up starting his own firm, Rebus Creative, doing across-the-board marketing and communications focused on not-for-profits, arts groups, and more: Brian put me on a retainer for my first year.

"Once I'd started getting that regular income and dedicating myself to this alternate career, things just started to snowball. I'm at the point now where I'd be very hard-pressed to take on even one more client! If I had any fears about it, that it was something I was doing just for the money, they're alleviated. I find I get such a charge out of seeing artists promoted in papers and on television shows. To see the richness of local people in the artistic community—it's so vital to get the message out to people. Of course, we want to hear about artists in LA and New York—it inspires us—we need to foster the growth of our local talent.

"It's so much fun, and to connect our media with the value I see in the arts—I guess that's what's really connected to MY initial urge, that love of acting. For me, it wasn't really standing onstage, it came from a love of reading, a love of words, and the effect that words and philosophy wrapped up in a stage production. The audience bears witness—and the power of that is so incredible. It's a total thrill to share that with people who read about (the artists I represent) in the local paper. It's like having the best dinner party, and everyone loves our food.

"I'm working with Circle Craft Cooperative; it's one of the largest craft cooperatives in North America. They're a wonderful group founded by a lady from Denmark in the seventies, who brought that country's notions of arts guilds with her when she moved here. It started in a little church basement, and now it's in our great big trade and convention center. I publicize their event every year, and 40,000 people come. I also work with a lot of writers; I just finished a big book festival down in Vancouver, and tens of thousands of people come to that. I work with the BC Book Prizes, the Western Magazine Awards, so much more!

"My goal with publicity is to be able to direct a team of publicists, and hopefully bring more people into this career, because I think it's a wonderful form of advocacy for the arts. It's a way to expand the landscape. Sir John Gielgud referred to theater as 'the outback of the entertainment industry.' So we need advocates on our side for theater, too! People have no idea what hard work theater is—you're expected to have a business brain, and an entertainment brain.

"When I first graduated from university, I went to a tarot card reader. He laid out the cards and wanted to me to ask him one question internally, but not tell him what it was. At the ending of the reading, he said, 'I can't answer your question, because you don't know its meaning. Until you do, you'll never find the answer.' My question was, 'When will I find success?'

"Success didn't come in the form of above-and-beyond recognition, although I've gotten some of that, and it is nice. It comes from connecting with my passions that I've fostered since I was old enough to know what I was doing, and seeing how those passions play out in my life, and how I can advance the things that are important to me.

"I've got a tremendous amount of energy inherited from my mom, from my Celtic roots. I feel like a terrier—once I get an idea, I just wrassle it! If you're not connected with your bliss, whatever it is that lights up life for you, I can see how that could lead to tremendous burnout. It could leave you without energy for life in general.

"One thing we forget about performing artists, about even the stars of Canadian and American stage, is that those people go from gig to gig. Each gig may last eight weeks, or a couple months at the most, and after that they're unemployed. They may not be able to collect unemployment insurance; they may have no medical or dental coverage. While it's vital to have your head in the clouds and get in touch with your dreams, it's also pretty important to have your feet on the ground, and look after your physical self. I think that was something I missed from my initial enthusiasm to throw myself into the creative arts. I don't think I measure my success by the money I make, but I definitely have had a great feeling seeing my bank account beef up, and paying off my student loans.

"Don't be afraid to ask for what you want, in negotiating what it is you need. Don't think what you're going to get by what you think you can have. I do that with publicity, too, and with shows I've worked on. I sit down and say, what do I want this to look like at the end? Then I build it backwards. It would be very wise to plan a career the same way. How would you like this to play out in the end? What kind of experiences would you like to be having in terms of getting the day job that's going to really get things moving for you?

"Each one of my clients brings me a new thrill, whether it's getting their glasswork on the front of the arts section in color, or introducing them to their fans. One highlight of the past year was taking Lynn Johnson, creator of the comic strip "For Better or For Worse," around to some media engagements. The line-ups of people to meet her, and the personal connections that they all had with her through her strip! I could have bawled my eyes out. At one point, this young girl came up to where Lynn was signing lithographs she's donated for literacy. The girl said, 'I just want to thank you for teaching my dad not to be homophobic.' I was like, wow!

"Because my clients are so diverse, that's the fun part about my day. Yesterday I worked in my home office, and I did work in my PJs for a while. My husband went out and bought me a latte and a bran muffin—I'd recommend that to anyone! Most of the time, though, I go down to my office in this great space in the Heritage building in downtown Vancouver. At Rebus, we're all doing something different—writing grants, marketing, we've got interns bringing new energy. It's great because we can spin off of each other, and if we have questions, like if I have problems with the computer!

"When I undertake a publicity push, I start off by researching my topic. I dig around, I go to the library, I constantly rely on the Internet—it's a great tool. I call the artists and actors and talk to them one on one. Often, people don't realize what's exciting about them, or what the media might find interesting. I cook up little story lines or pitches, fire them out to all my friends in the media by e-mail. Once I get really confident, I start leaving phone messages. I might do that for weeks, yet with another project I'm at a different stage, so I've got to juggle that, too. Suddenly the media are coming back to me, saying, oh, that's a great story idea you had. They ask me to connect them with the artist.

"Now that I'm more successful, I'm writing my clients' campaigns simultaneously, while they are all at different stages of growth. If anybody had asked me if I thought I could do this before I started doing it, I don't think I would have thought I could do it. The computer is a tremendous tool, and enthusiasm for your subject, whatever it is, is your best ally."

THE SELF-MADE MAN

James O'Regan's talent and tenacity truly marks him as an artistic jack-of-all trades—and a very savvy businessman. Starting off as a student of liturgy, O'Regan became a journeyman actor in his native Canada; his resume quickly filled up with roles in movies, TV, and commercials for clients such as Radio Shack and Stroh's Beer. Once he'd become one of his country's most recognizable faces, O'Regan's next plan of action was to get a pet personal project produced—the dream of many an actor, and one that often goes unrealized.

Not in O'Regan's case. He figured out the system, and produced his own film, *Edsville*, which enjoyed a successful run in both Canadian theaters and on TV. O'Regan is now constantly busy working on future comedy features. Here he offers both words of inspiration—and some good old-fashioned practical truths—for those who'd like to grab hold of their creative and business lives as fruitfully as he did.

How I Got the Ball Rolling

"*Edsville* came to me as I was walking down the street to an audition in Toronto. It came with a title and about ninety seconds of action—initially, a one-joke premise. The original screenplay featured the legs of a man, in gray suit pants, walking down the sidewalk. At that level, he passes a dog dressed in a gray suit. The camera pans up to reveal the chap as he passes into an old-fashioned general store. We see the back of a clerk; we hear off-camera, 'Scuse me?', whereupon the clerk fiddles with his hair, shrugs up his shoulders, turns, and does an Ed Sullivan impersonation. We cut to the customer, also an Ed Sullivan impersonator. They transact a simple purchase, then the customer leaves; as he walks down the sidewalk, everyone we see is an Ed Sullivan impersonator. Fade to black. Pretty simple, and could be shot in half a day.

"That [the idea] did pop into my mind was probably a function of director Alan Marr and I fooling around on set and in auditions as 'Ed Sullivans'; we had been doing that for a couple of years. After my audition that day, I walked straight over to Alan's studio and said, 'Let's shoot *Edsville*.' Alan agreed, spoke to a director of photography, Harry Lake, who also agreed, and within minutes we had one of the best commercial crews in Canada willing and able to work on it. Alan, Stu Chow, another pal, and I fleshed out those ninety seconds into a 'Twilight Zone'-type scenario that became the script; Kathleen Laskey provided improvised dialogue for the opening sequence [during shooting].

"Originally, I had wanted to find a producer. While I was searching, I started to take care of pre-production, looking for markets and money, as well as location scouting and casting. Out of the blue, I got a GM car commercial campaign that paid about $10,000. I could afford film and meals, so we started to shoot, with me as de facto producer, and Dan Ford as line producer—he's simply the best and actually did all the nuts and bolts work."

Master of the Master Plan

"Because this type of production had not been done before within AFTRA jurisdiction, I had to come up with a legal and corporate scenario that would satisfy everyone. I worked up a spreadsheet that distributed shares to all willing cast, crew, and suppliers, to pay down their own promissory notes to invest in our company A Really Big Production, Inc., with labor at standard daily rates. That aggregate, with a few additions, became my budget of $120,000, accounting for 120,000 shares valued at $1 each.

"Now all contributors were owners of the film. It looked on the surface like deferred payments, and acted like it in terms of cash flow, but all the owners were in a legal position to know what was what. Our company paid out $16,000 in revenues to its shareholders within two years."

The Joy of Selling

"I spent a year, in the days before the Internet and e-mail, marketing the film in all windows. The highlights included *Edsville* becoming the first short film in Canada to earn box office revenue by playing in repertory cinemas. The film played after a feature with which it was coupled—a different feature in each cinema. Patrons paid an extra dollar to see both a feature and *Edsville*, and if they wished to leave before *Edsville*, they were refunded the dollar. Ten thousand patrons paid to see *Edsville*, and our company made $5,000. That was my first creative business move, in my first opportunity to be responsible for and do actual business."

Know Your Worth

"*Edsville* opened the Toronto Film Festival with rave reviews, and went on to play a dozen or so festivals worldwide. It won a gold medal [at a festival] in Spain, and was picked up by Finnish TV as a result of the Tampere short film fest.

"I had originally taken the script to the Canadian Broadcasting Company in 1989 [before producing it myself], asking for $4,000 [to film it]. They turned me down. After it had played at the Toronto Film Festival, however, I started getting calls from the CBC—they wanted to buy the film. I refused, because the TV window was [still] down the line, and I had yet to fully exploit cinema and video. After a year of calls, I finally said they could have it for January 1992. Our deal ended up costing them almost four times what they could have had it for in 1989.

That one lesson taught me that if all possible, hold on to risk and to leverage, but be prepared to live with good or bad consequences."

Well-Earned Wisdom

"Find creative and resourceful collaborators who follow your vision, and correct it when necessary. Then, just do [your project] with whatever resources are handy. *Edsville* today would have cost much less because shooting has evolved. We shot on 35 mm, although we edited on non-linear software, then in the early days of development.

"Watch, listen, ask questions, make sure you understand what it is you don't yet know, and then give that [unfamiliar thing] a try. Nothing is guaranteed. Be wary of distribution and exhibition. If you can, hold on to your leverage until the right deal comes forward, but know that at some point, you must let the project go into other hands. Just make sure those hands know what they're doing, and that you retain control of your project by cash flow and rights reserved. We turned down Disney and the Comedy Channel because their offers were pitifully low; [going with] a big player doesn't mean a thing if it's not going to treat your project right.

"Lastly, be persistent. Last one standing wins."

THE NATURE OF NURTURE

In the rough-and-tumble film and theater world, a compassionate casting director seems like the ultimate oxymoron. However, JT Wagner's innate understanding of the actor's psyche turns this assumption completely on its ear.

The daughter of award-winning Broadway set designer Alex Toland, Wagner's acting career was set in motion by the legendary Lee Strasberg, with whom she studied extensively. She has worked constantly as an actress onstage in New York (*Sweet Bird of Youth*, *Orpheus Descending*, and *The Effect of Gamma Rays on Man-in-the-Moon Marigolds* are just a few of her credits) and in film. As a teacher, her Stanislavski technique–based theory has been offered at prestigious training institutes like Weist-Barron-Ryan, the Village East Workshop, and Terra Cottage in South Hampton, New York. She's also an experienced director.

Wagner's heavy-duty connections in the film and theater communities have helped make her reputation as a crackerjack casting director as well. In addition to her ability to connect actors with top directors and producers, actors whom she casts love her for another reason—she feels their pain. She has tremendous empathy for the intense preparation, guts, and leap-of-faith dedication showing up for that audition truly takes. Wagner's commitment to showing her appreciation for an actor's effort truly set her apart from the pack. These are her rules for developing a successful casting approach.

One: Learn from Those Who Have Gone Before You

"I don't think I can remember how or when I decided to become an actor. It picked me; I didn't pick it. My education was intensive—performing arts school, years at Lee Strasberg, extensive scene study at the Actors' Studio. The Method and the people who shaped my life saved my life. I was an angry young woman who was, in my opinion, going nowhere, until I discovered the power of my own creativity. I don't think I would have made it this far, if it wasn't for the unique people who helped me—Geraldine Page, Lee Strasberg, Shelley Winters, Burgess Meredith, Anna Strasberg, Irma Saundry. [Now] my philosophy for my work and life is to be humble in a competitive world, and to love the art in myself, not myself in the art."

Two: Exercise Empathy

"I began to realize that being an actress was not going to be enough, in terms of what my destiny was. When I graduated from the Lee Strasberg Institute, I wanted to act and teach, but more than that, I wanted to help other actors. So in conjunction with my work as an actress/director/teacher of the Method, I became friendly with casting people. I've been doing this work since—and I have found my calling! What a joy—to help actors who have been abused by people in the business."

Three: See Beyond the Surface

"At times, the people who you think will never be right for the part ARE, and everything seems topsy-turvy! I can usually tell a good actor by the way they first present themselves at an audition. Weakness for film is not a plus unless the character is a weak one, and even then, we need a strong actor to interpret that weakness."

Four: Be Truly Proud of Your Performers

"When I see the light go on in an actor's face when they get a part, for me, it's very rewarding, because I know what that feeling is. I've presented awards to actors that I myself have had a hand in shaping, and this is a great personal achievement."

Five: Failure Helps You Flourish

"It is my experience that I have never played a role or directed or been involved in a piece that wasn't fraught with regrets, rejection, or butting of creative minds. I've never learned from good things that I've been involved with, however. So my advice to young actors is, enjoy the rejection! You don't really know if any experience is good until it's finished, and you've already moved on to the next project."

Six: Keep Taking Risks

"If you do what you've always done, you'll get what you've always gotten."

THE WIZARD OF IMPROV

When David Christopher couldn't find the job he wanted, he defined and created it himself—and started an empire. Christopher founded Just The Funny, an interactive, improv-based corporate services company in Miami. JTF provides both performers and original performance pieces to help corporations market products, sell at trade shows, and promote their services. Additionally, Christopher and his team innovated a unique business training model called BizProv, which facilitates actual actor-improv training workshops to help corporate employees become more effective and creative in terms of generating and carrying out work projects. The company also specializes in teambuilding through improv technique. The pay-off: satisfied clients include Direct TV, Honeywell, Bell South, and Clear Channel.

Christopher is also deeply committed to providing great live improv entertainment to Miami audiences through JTF's live performances and improv festival. He talks about the road he's traveled with the company so far, and where he plans to go in the future.

On Beginnings

"I was born and raised in Miami, and got a BFA in film from New York University. I lived in New York for quite a while, and did film and television for quite a long time. I came back to Miami to shoot a film, funding fell through, and I found myself out of work. That's when I started doing improv. I then went on to more film and TV—I produced the series *Blind Date*—and then I had my daughter, and just changed.my priorities. I realized a lot of what I was doing wasn't really good for family life, so I went back to school and got an MBA, and started doing corporate improv.

"I started Just The Funny back in 1999, with a number of other actors. We just wanted to go ahead and do improv the way we wanted to do it—long-form, short-form, and really, just be able to branch out, and eventually grow the business."

On Development

"With Just The Funny, the biggest challenge IS just growing the business. We started out with nothing; we didn't have a cent in the bank. We were like guerilla business people, running around handing out flyers; we were like a rock band on the LA strip, trying to get people to come to our performances! Now, we are definitely the leaders in our market here in Miami. We've done this through a lot of hard work, and by being open, listening to our people. We've really taken a sound look at how we were structured as an organization, because we really value our people. Our people are our product."

On Doing the Job

"Our approach to corporate improv is definitely an analytical one. When you're doing improvisation, you're really trained to listen, to pay attention to your surroundings, to pick up things that are going on. You have to pick up key pieces of information and be able to use them. You have to be an observer and a communicator. Those are two skill sets that are really transferable to anything in life, and definitely to the business world.

"How I explain (to clients) how improv can benefit in the business world is, basically, that in improv, we're trying to recreate life. In improv, we have to be the writer and the actor at the same time, and you don't get a second chance. That's exactly how it is in life; everybody's constantly improvising, whether it's a business or personal situation. What I really push for is for clients to look at life through the same glasses as an improviser would. My job is to facilitate, get people to understand the rules, fundamentals and ideas of improv, and be able to apply it to what they do.

"In most sessions, I do more role-playing than anything else; it's very interactive. What I do is find out ahead of time, what challenges are facing the organization? Why are they hiring us in the first place, and what are they trying to achieve? Then I dissect what's at the root of the problem by role-playing with all the key players in the organization. I generally try to keep supervisors and decision-makers out of this process—we can do something separate with them, but I try to keep [supervised workers] open, comfortable, and feeling that it's OK to fail. That's something that we learn in improv—that failure is OK, and it's going to happen in life. The stress, nervousness, and tension that comes from fear of failure, a lot of times, keeps people from succeeding. We work on situations more than once, using the group experience, because the group can really shed some light. So that's why I really consider myself more of a facilitator. I'm there to help them play the game, to understand what improv's all about, to force them up onstage."

On Results

"Once they do a scene, it's like magic. Everybody gets into it, and they realize, 'We're not being asked to act, or made to look like fools. We're being asked to try different approaches to resolve conflicts, increasing our communication at work.'

"I led a session where people were asked to write down their challenges. One twenty-one-year-old woman wrote that she'd never interviewed for what she called a 'real' job, with a resume, and how would she present herself. She wanted to confront that. It just so happened that right there [in the session], we had a VP of marketing, who used to be in human resources. So we teamed them up onstage, and the professional interviewed her. I said, 'Give her her worst-case scenario.' She had a horrible interview; it was a complete failure. But then everybody gave her feedback, very supportively and constructively. The professional in the improv gave this young woman all the tips that she needed to nail that NEXT interview. They did the role-play again, and this time she nailed the interview. She was able to spread her wings, and just go for it!"

On the Big Picture

"I'm known as the one in our group with like, this uber-drive. I'm extremely focused and detail-oriented and a perfectionist, and I drive everybody crazy with that! My goal for the company is to open up our own venue; to offer a full training center.

"We're members of the chamber of commerce; we're very active in the community, and do a lot of charity work. I'm also extremely proud of our festival; the Miami Improv Festival is my personal baby. Without the festival, nobody would be doing long-form improvisation in Miami—nobody'd seen it, nobody understood it. That just exploded the scene down here. We've grown the audience to support it, and I'm most proud of the fact that we've kind of put Miami and South Florida on the map. I'm glad to help out other improv groups down here, too.

"It's not about being the best in a small pond, it's about, let's grow the pond, and worry about our market share later."

STAYING TRUE TO YOU

All of the people in this book spend their lives striving for goals. Some started with one goal, and never lost sight of it; some segued with enthusiasm from one track to another; many more struggled when they had to give up a long held dream and set their sight on another goal. But all of them have held onto their determination to define—and live—successful, happy lives. So should you. And what is your most important objective, no matter who you are? Your first loyalty must always be to take care of yourself.

Sounds like a no-brainer, right? But for many performers, self-preservation is actually the toughest nut to crack. Actors are taught to give everything they've got away—to whatever production they happen to be working on, to their fellow cast members, to art as a whole out of respect for all serious thespians who came before them throughout the history of humankind. You're supposed to sweat, bleed, and go onstage even though you just passed a kidney stone and you haven't had the money to eat for two days. To that I say—baloney.

Your first obligation should always be to your personal care, safety, and security, whether you're a working actor or pursuing another profession. (And if you've got a family to feed, clothe, and shelter, that first obligation multiplies.) Sacrifice may be noble, but when you get right down to brass tacks, it's not a whole lot of fun. Besides, who can do ANY job well if their physical and emotional comfort is continually compromised?

The theater, film, and TV business can provide you with wonderful benefits and even riches if you're lucky, but it does not have your best interest at heart. It's a numbers game, where everybody's replaceable. To prove this point, actor friends of mine play a game called "I'm The New Blank." Simply think of a famous actor or actress from days gone by, and then think of the counterpart who's replaced this person in the public eye today. Example: Brad Pitt is the new Robert Redford. Angelina Jolie is the new Elizabeth Taylor. Jennifer Aniston is the new Mary Tyler Moore. You get the gist— the business breaks down into a few archetypes that spin themselves forward endlessly. And sooner or later, a new face always takes over. So maybe YOU should take care not to invest your entire, beautiful, irreplaceable heart and soul into a machine that you can only expect so much from in the end, no matter WHO you are.

If you want to be an actor, decide what portion of your life pie you can truly afford to dedicate to your goal. To do this, make sure the following needs are always taken care of first:

1. Your health. You need health insurance, a doctor, enough money to eat a healthy diet, stay warm in the winter, and properly clothe yourself.
2. Your shelter. Couch-surfing does not count in this category. You need your own secure rooms, apartment or home.
3. Your happiness. A life of constant audition rejection numbs you intensely. You were put on earth to feel joy, you know! It's OK to feel good OUTSIDE of those times you've just booked

a commercial, landed a lead, or enjoyed a standing ovation—those professional moments are great, but pretty fleeting too when you think about it.

4. Your luxuries. And creature comfort to me is a NEED. You deserve to enjoy a nice dinner out, buy that designer handbag, or go on a super vacation from time to time. Treating yourself well feeds your self-esteem, just as healthy food nourishes your body. If you're counting out pennies to see if you can afford to splurge on that latte at Starbucks, it's time to rethink the game plan.

Whatever energy and resources you've got left after you take care of these needs you can and should commit fully to your acting aspirations. And you know what? If you take care of your physical and mental well-being first and foremost, you'll find you have MORE energy and resources to commit than ever, because you'll be happy and rested and well-fed. You'll be able to think better, and that always leads to new, exciting avenues toward success.

So to meet your needs, and ultimately, become a better actor, you need gainful employment that gives you satisfaction. No matter what kind of employment that happens to be. Once you've figured out the alternate way you want to make a living, while contributing something great to the world, life becomes so much more peaceful.

And you know what? You might actually find you prefer another career to acting, when all is said and done. That's OK. Life is all about new discovery. You don't have to bury your old dreams permanently—your art will always be there for you in some way, shape or form whenever you might want to go back to it.

Just take care of yourself first, and everything will work out fine.

support organizations

The following organizations can assist actors with career change information, guidance, employer networking, financial/legal concerns, and/or benefit information.

The Actors' Work Program, New York/The Actors' Fund
729 Seventh Avenue
New York, NY 10019
(212) 354-5480
www.actorsfund.org

The Actors' Work Program, Los Angeles/The Actors' Fund
5757 Wilshire Blvd., Suite 400
Los Angeles, CA
(323) 933-9244 ext. 50
www.actorsfund.org

An actor's greatest resource for career direction, development, support, and skill-building.

The Foundation Center
79 Fifth Avenue
New York, NY 10003
(212) 620-4230
www.fdncenter.org

The definitive resource for information as it applies to grant money for artists.

Volunteer Lawyers for the Arts
1 East 53rd Street
6th Floor
New York, NY 10022
(212) 319-2787 (information directory)
(212) 319-2910 (legal matters line)
(212) 752-6575 (fax)
www.vlany.org (e-mail vlany@bway.net)

The industry standard for providing legal information and assistance at no cost to the artist.

national service organizations

Here is a listing of some national service organizations you may wish to contact for arts-related career resource information.

Americans for the Arts (New York City)
1 East 53rd Street
New York, NY 10022
(212) 223-2787
(212) 753-1325
www.artsusa.org

Americans for the Arts (Washington, DC)
1000 Vermont Avenue NW
12th Floor
Washington, DC 20005
(202) 371-2830
(202) 371-0424 (fax)

A top-notch artist support/resource organization.

American Theater Wing
250 West 57th Street
Suite 519
New York, NY 10107
(212) 869-5470

Education, theater history, preservation, and a great wealth of information for any artist.

Black Theatre Network
c/o Kuntu Rep Theatre, 3T01 Wesley W. Posvar Hall
230 S. Bouguet Street
Pittsburgh, PA 15260
rroebuck@pitt.edu

A very well-respected educational/professional service link-up.

Institute of Outdoor Drama
CB#3240
University of North Carolina
Chapel Hill, NC 27599-3240
(919) 962-1328
(919) 962-4212 (fax)
outdoor@unc.edu (e-mail)
www.unc.edu/depts/outdoor

Information and resources about and for US outdoor theaters, including a national directory of venues.

The League of American Theatres and Producers
226 West 47th Street
New York, NY 10036
(212) 764-1122

An important resource for arts administrators.

National Endowment for the Arts
1100 Pennsylvania Avenue NW
Washington, DC 20506
(202) 682-5400
www.nea.gov

The preeminent national government organization for arts funding. In addition to information about the organization and FAQs, the Web site supplies grant application guidelines.

Performing Arts Resources
dbradypar@aol.com
http://Members.aol.com/perfrtsrc

A membership community linking up artists with job resources and more.

Stage Managers Association
PO Box 275
Times Square Station
New York, NY 10108-2020
(212) 543-9567
www.stagemanagers.org

Networking and trouble-shooting for stage managers.

Theatre Communications Group (TCG)
355 Lexington Avenue
4th Floor
New York, NY 1007
(212) 697-5230
www.tcg.org

Publisher of *American Theater* magazine, as well as *ArtSearch*, the bimonthly employment bulletin for people in the arts, TCG also produces books and directories, presents grants and internships, and offers guidance, support, and information for professional theaters and theater professionals throughout the country.

Theatre Development Fund
1501 Broadway
21st Floor
New York, NY 10036
(212) 221-0885
www.tdf.org

TDF offers discount tickets through a membership program and also through its famous **TKTS®** discount ticket booths in Times Square and South Street Seaport. TDF also administers a range of audience development and financial assistance programs that encourage production of new plays.

University/Resident Theatre Association
1560 Broadway
Suite 141
New York, NY 10036
(212) 221-1130
(212) 869-2752 (fax)
URTA@aol.com
www.URTA.com

The University/Resident Theatre Association is the country's oldest and largest consortium of professional theater training graduate programs and associated professional theater companies. U/RTA encourages the professional training of artists, and of future teachers in the performing arts for all levels of education.

United States Institute for Theatre Technology
6443 Ridings Road
Syracuse, NY 13206-1111
(315) 463-6463
(315) 463-6525
www.USITT.org

United States Institute for Theatre Technology, Inc. (USITT) is the association of design, production, and technology professionals in the performing arts and entertainment industry. The mission of USITT is to actively promote the advancement of the knowledge and skills of its members.

Appendix C
unions

Here is a round-up of the major theatrical union organizations across the US. If you're an artist on the cusp of a new career direction, make sure to consult with your applicable union in regard to health benefits, salary, and unemployment questions and issues.

Actors Equity Association (National Headquarters)
165 West 46th Street
New York, NY 10036
(212) 869-8530
www.actorsequity.org

Actors Equity Association (Los Angeles)
5757 Wilshire Blvd.
Suite 1
Los Angeles, CA 90036
(323) 634-1750

Actors Equity Association (Chicago)
203 North Wabash Avenue
Suite 1700
Chicago, IL 60601
(312) 641-0393

Actors Equity Association (San Francisco)
235 Pine Street
Suite 1200
San Francisco, CA 94104
(415) 391-3838

Actors Equity Association (Orlando, Florida)
10369 Orangewood Boulevard
Orlando, FL 32821
(407) 345-8600

American Guild of Variety Artists
184 Fifth Avenue
6th Floor
New York, NY 10010
(212) 675-1003
http://americanguildofvarietyartistsagva.visualnet.com/

Association of Authors' Representatives
10 Astor Place
3rd Floor
New York, NY 10003
(212) 353-3709
www.aar-online.org

The Dramatists Guild, Inc.
234 West 44th Street
New York, NY 10036
(212) 398-9366
www.dramaguild.com

Society of Stage Directors and Choreographers
1501 Broadway
17th Floor
New York, NY 10036
(212) 391-1070
www.ssdc.org

Appendix D
membership
associations

The following associations can be helpful in terms of providing work facilitations and networking for arts professionals.

American Music Center (AMC)
30 West 26th Street, Suite 1001
New York, NY 10010-2011
(212) 366-5260
www.amc.net

A great resource for those transitioning into music careers.

American Translators Association
225 Reinekers Ln., Suite 590
Alexandria, VA 22314-2840
(703) 683-6100
www.atanet.org

Membership organization with information and career resources for translators.

Association for Theatre in Higher Education
Box 69
Downers Grove, IL 60515-0069
(888) 284-3737
www.athe.org

The Association for Theatre in Higher Education is an organization of individuals and institutions that provides vision and leadership for the profession and promotes excellence in theater education.

The Field
161 Sixth Avenue
New York, NY 10013
(212) 691-6969
www.thefield.org

The Field offers programs that help independent artists create new artwork, manage their careers, and develop long-range strategies for sustaining a life in the arts.

PEN American Center
568 Broadway
New York, NY 10012
(212) 334-1660
www.pen.org

An organization that stands for freedom of speech, and offers fellowship and support to writers.

web career resources

The following Internet sites can provide detailed information on locating employment in numerous fields.

The Actor's Checklist
www.actorschecklist.com

American Theatre Resources
www.theatre-resources.net

ArtsLynx International Theatre Resources
www.artslynx.com

Career Builder
www.careerbuilder.com

Career Journal
www.careerjournal.com

The Casting Network
www.thecastingnetwork.com

Craig's List
www.craigslist.com

High Tech New York
www.hightechny.com

Hot Jobs
www.hotjobs.com

Jobs.com
www.jobs.com

Monster.com
www.monster.com

New York Business
www.newyorkbusiness.com

NY Career Zone
www.nycareerzone.org

Playbill Online
www.playbill.com

Variety Careers
www.varietycareers.com

publications

Consult the following publications for consistently helpful information about general career issues and the business of entertainment. Subscription contact info is listed below; also check newsstands for a number of these titles.

ArtSearch
c/o Theatre Communications Group
355 Lexington Avenue
New York, NY 10017
(212) 697-5230
www.tcg.com

Subscription and Web subscription publication that provides job leads for people in the arts.

Back Stage/Back Stage West/Drama-Logue
1-800-437-3183
www.backstage.com

The entertainment industry newspaper for actors. Audition listings, plus current news about "actor-centric" aspects of show business, and career advice.

Black Talent News
8306 Wilshire Blvd. Suite 2057
Beverly Hills, CA 90211
(301) 203-1336
www.blacktalentnews.com

Dramatics Magazine/Teaching Theatre
Educational Theatre Association
2343 Auburn Avenue
Cincinnati, OH 45219-2815
www.edta.org

Magazines for theater students and educators.

Equal Opportunity
Equal Opportunity Publications, Inc.
445 Broad Hollow Rd., Suite 425
Melville, NY 11747
www.eop.com

Publishes career magazines for women, members of minority groups, and people with disabilities.

Hollywood Reporter
5055 Wilshire Boulevard
Los Angeles, CA 90036
(213) 525-2000
www.hollywoodreporter.com

The entertainment industry trade magazine.

Stage Directions Magazine
110 William Street, 23rd Floor
New York, NY 10031
www.stage-directions.com

A magazine about theatrical production, largely technical, and aimed at regional, community, and school theaters.

Theatrical Index
888 Eighth Avenue
New York, NY 10019
(212) 585-6343

Theatrical Index is filled with information on musicals, plays scheduled to open, and current theatrical offerings. Specifically geared to professionals within the theater industry, it contains information on producers, agents, and publicists.

Variety/Daily Variety
5700 Wilshire Boulevard
Suite 120
Los Angeles, CA 90036-5804
(323) 965-4476

Entertainment industry news. Statistics, reviews, and columns.

index

Books from Allworth Press

Allworth Press is an imprint of Allworth Communications, Inc. Selected titles are listed below.

Acting Is a Job: Real Life Lessons about the Acting Business
by Jason Pugatch (paperback, 6 × 9, 240 pages, $19.95)

The Actor's Way: A Journey of Self-Discovery in Letters
by Benjamin Lloyd (paperback, 5 ½ × 8 ½, 224 pages, $16.95)

Letters from Backstage: The Adventures of a Touring Stage Actor
by Michael Kostroff (paperback, 6 × 9, 224 pages, $16.95)

Making It on Broadway: Actors' Tales of Climbing to the Top
by David Wienir and Jodie Langel (paperback, 6 × 9, 288 pages, $19.95)

An Actor's Guide—Making It in New York City
by Glenn Alterman (paperback, 6 × 9, 288 pages, $19.95)

The Art of Auditioning: Techniques for Television
by Rob Decina (paperback, 6 × 9, 224 pages, $19.95)

An Actor Rehearses: What to Do When—and Why
by David Hlavsa (paperback, 6 × 9, 208 pages, $18.95)

Improv for Actors
by Dan Diggles (paperback, 6 × 9, 256 pages, $19.95)

Acting—Advanced Techniques for the Actor, Director, and Teacher
by Terry Schreiber (paperback, 6 × 9, 256 pages, $19.95)

Promoting Your Acting Career: A Step-by-Step Guide to Opening the Right Doors, Second Edition
by Glen Alterman (paperback, 6 × 9, 240 pages, $19.95)

Acting that Matters
by Barry Pineo (paperback, 5 ½ × 8 ½, 240 pages, $16.95)

VO: Tales and Techniques of a Voice-Over Actor
by Harlan Hogan (paperback, 6 × 9, 256 pages, $19.95)

Please write to request our free catalog. To order by credit card, call 1-800-491-2808 or send a check or money order to Allworth Press, 10 East 23rd Street, Suite 510, New York, NY 10010. Include $6 for shipping and handling for the first book ordered and $1 for each additional book. Eleven dollars plus $1 for each additional book if ordering from Canada. New York State residents must add sales tax.

To see our complete catalog on the World Wide Web, or to order online, you can find us at **www.allworth.com.**